The Spirituality of the Gospels

THE
SPIRITUALITY
OF THE
GOSPELS

STEPHEN C. BARTON

Wipf & Stock
PUBLISHERS
Eugene, Oregon

Wipf and Stock Publishers
199 W 8th Ave, Suite 3
Eugene, OR 97401

The Spirituality of the Gospels
By Barton, Stephen C.
Copyright©1992 by Barton, Stephen C.
ISBN: 1-59752-909-5
Publication date: 1/16/2005
Previously published by SPCK, 1992

To Fiona
and to my mother
and
in memory of
my father

CONTENTS

Preface   ix

Introduction   1

1 *'You therefore must be perfect, as your heavenly Father
is perfect'*
   The Spirituality of Matthew   9

2 *'For everyone will be salted with fire'*
   The Spirituality of Mark   39

3 *'You will have joy and gladness'*
   The Spirituality of Luke-Acts   71

4 *'You will know the truth and the truth will make you free'*
   The Spirituality of the Fourth Gospel   113

Conclusion   144

Bibliography   149

Index   159

PREFACE

The immediate origin of this book was an invitation to deliver four lectures at the Vacation Term for Biblical Studies at St Anne's College, Oxford, at the end of July 1991. Having studied and taught the gospels for about ten years, the invitation to deliver four lectures suggested immediately that I devote one lecture to each gospel. I thought it would be worthwhile to try to convey to the best of my ability what I had come to understand each of the canonical gospels to be *really* about. A naïve intention, of course—especially when the study of any single text or passage or theme in the gospels is virtually inexhaustible, and more and more monographs are being written from ever-increasing points of view on smaller and smaller pieces of text!

Nevertheless, there is something to be said for taking stock every now and then, and for standing back and getting the wider view of the whole. In particular, because the gospels are written from faith for faith, it seems legitimate to try to grasp what they are saying about life under God or life lived in response to the sense of the presence of God—specifically, the presence of God revealed in Jesus Christ through the Spirit. So I entitled the lectures, *The Spirituality of the Gospels*. I am much indebted to the Committee of the V.T.B.S. for extending the invitation and for the marvellous care and hospitality the members showed to me during the conference itself.

But my debts for this my first book go much further. Amongst my New Testament teachers in three universities, I would mention particularly Edwin Judge, Robert Banks, David Catchpole and Graham Stanton. Then must come the students I have taught at Bishop Otter College and the Theological College in Chichester, at Salisbury and Wells Theological College in Salisbury, and now at the Department of Theology in the University of Durham. At

PREFACE

Salisbury, I was encouraged and enabled to make connections between academic biblical study and the life of a worshipping community of ordinands and their families. That is where spirituality and the concept of spiritual formation became important to me. Here I would acknowledge especially the friendship and stimulus of Trevor Dennis, Ruth Siddals, Alan Gregory and Nicholas Bradbury, and the support of the then Principal, Reginald Askew. Since coming to Durham, I have been very privileged to work in such a graceful environment and such a lively theology department. To Ann Loades and to the university authorities, thanks are due for the sabbatical term which made possible the writing of these lectures. Jimmy Dunn and Sandy Wedderburn have been extremely supportive colleagues in New Testament Studies and in the intricacies of computing. Walter Moberly has encouraged me most to take seriously the fact that the gospels are a central part of what Christians call 'Holy Scripture' and have their true place in enlivening and sustaining communities of faith. These lectures owe a lot to his critical eye and to conversations with him. Special thanks are due also to Leslie Houlden and Gordon Mursell, for their friendship, their own writing in the area of biblical spirituality and for giving these lectures a critical reading.

To George Hepburn and Jan McGregor, who allowed the Barton family to mind their house and dog over the Easter vacation of 1991, when the lectures were given their penultimate form, many thanks. Nor could I fail to mention with deep gratitude my parents-in-law Stanley and Gladys Giltrap, and also Richard and Clare Firth, Sue Bowder and all the members of St John's Church, Neville's Cross, whose practical and spiritual support during an extended period of serious illness in the family allowed life to go on almost as normal. Above all, however, I would like to thank my wife, Fiona, our four children, Anna, Thomas, Joseph and Miriam, and my father and mother, George and Nancy Barton. Unfortunately, my father died before seeing this book. It is to Fiona and my mother and the memory of my father that the book is dedicated.

Stephen C. Barton
Durham
Lent 1992

INTRODUCTION

What is Christian spirituality? For some, especially in the Catholic tradition and those influenced by it, spirituality is about prayer, meditation, confession, making retreats, and ascetical practices such as fasting; and it is where a spiritual director properly trained in the disciplines of the soul plays an important role. For others, perhaps from a more Protestant tradition, spirituality is basically about the joyful experience of justification and conversion along with their consequences for ethics and daily discipleship, and intimations of the cloister or the idea of priestly direction in the life of the soul have little appeal. Each of these models—sketched all too superficially, of course—has its strength and profundity, as well as its shortcomings. The 'Catholic' model is strong in its tradition of withdrawal and in its long practice of the spiritual disciplines, but weak perhaps in its ability to translate its vitality beyond the sphere of the cloister and the full-time 'religious'. The 'Protestant' model is strong in its ability to engage lay people in their life in the everyday world, but weak perhaps in its disparagement of tradition, 'religion' and the mystical, and in its tendency towards activism and individualism.

The study which follows works with neither of these models and, instead, tries to go behind them to a biblical under-standing—maybe in a way which will speak to those who identify with one or the other, or with a different model altogether. In simplest terms, spirituality as I use it in this book has to do with *the sense of the divine presence and living in the light of that presence*. There are two basic aspects therefore: knowing and being known by God, on the one hand, and responding with the whole of life, on the other.[1] To put it another way, spirituality has to do with life under God: and for Christians, it has to do

1

specifically with life under the God who is revealed in Jesus and who graces believers with the Spirit. Clearly, this is a much broader definition of Christian spirituality than those described above. It is not, however, without its points of contact with both the 'Catholic' and the 'Protestant' approaches. Its advantage for this study of the gospels is that it does more justice to the originating moment' which they re-present, as we shall see.

The four gospels are classic expressions of Christian spirituality. That is the central theme of this book. They are shaped through and through by a sense of the presence of God in Christ, and they are deeply serious attempts to re-envisage the whole of life in response. Thus, for *Matthew*, Jesus is 'God with us' (Matt. 1.23), and life as the Israel of God and as the children of Abraham can never be the same again. The sense of fulfilment, of history at a turning-point, is overwhelming. In Jesus, the Son of God, heaven and earth have touched for salvation and judgment, and God's new people are brought into being to live as 'the light of the world' (Matt. 5.14). The message of *Mark*, similarly, is 'gospel', the 'good news' of Jesus Christ and of the coming of the reign of God (cf. Mark 1.1, 15). Above all, and most paradoxically, the sense of the divine presence is manifest in the messiah's cry of forsakenness on the cross (Mark 15.33–39). In consequence, the way of faith is the way of the cross which no true disciple may avoid. In *Luke-Acts*, too, there is a strong sense of 'the way' (cf. Luke 9.51ff.; Acts 9.2). Here, it is the joyous pilgrim way opened up by Jesus and his apostles in the power of God's Spirit. To go that way demands faith, repentance and perseverance. But the sense of God's presence is all-pervasive—in 'signs and wonders' and other revelations of divine power from beginning to end—so the ultimate outcome is not in doubt. Then there is the *Fourth Gospel*. And do we not have here pre-eminently a work vibrant with the testimony of witness after witness to the glory of God made known in Jesus the Son (cf. John 1.14)? And is not this extended meditation on God-in-Christ at the same time also an invitation to have 'eternal life' by believing in the Son and being 'born again' (cf. John 3)?

This is to anticipate what is to come in the succeeding chapters. But by doing so, I want to show that to inquire into the spirituality of the gospels is an appropriate thing to do. Indeed, perhaps it is the *most* appropriate thing to do especially if, as I would claim and as is recognized widely, the gospels are 'faith documents' from start to finish—written expressions of profound encounters with the divine, intended to mediate those experiences to others as the basis for faith, repentance and new life. The opening sentences of 1 John are apt evocations of what we find in the gospels and how we should come to them: 'That which was from the beginning, which we have heard, which we have seen with our eyes, which we have looked upon and touched with our hands, concerning the word of life . . . that which we have seen and heard we proclaim also to you . . .' (1.1–3).

Obviously, it is possible to read the gospels (or any of the biblical texts) for a variety of purposes. For instance, the gospels can be read as historical sources, where the aim is to see what light these ancient documents cast on Palestine under Roman occupation, the life of Jesus of Nazareth, the origins of Christianity, the beliefs and practices of the early church, and so on. This is a perfectly legitimate way of reading and has a distinguished pedigree. To some extent, the reading which I am going to give of the gospels is a reading which takes for granted an historical commitment of this kind. For I too am concerned to engage in an interpretation of the meaning of the gospel texts in their historical context, to describe with as much historical sensitivity as I can how the four evangelists envisaged life under God in the light of the coming of Christ. Furthermore, within the historical paradigm, the findings of redaction criticism—the investigation of the meaning of the gospel texts in their final form as compositions of the respective evangelists—are crucial for the present study.[2]

Nevertheless, historical investigation does not take us far enough. In particular, it tends to pay insufficient heed to the fact that the gospels are documents of the canon of Christian scripture held as sacred within the communities of Christian faith which scripture sustains and nourishes. Typically, historical method works by creating a critical distance between reader and text, whereas the expectation and hope of the believer is for inspiration and illumination in the life of faith, gained through a sympathetic proximity between reader and text. Awareness of this problem has led to attempts to take more seriously both the literary dimension of the gospels as texts to be read,[3] and also

3

the canonical context of the gospels, including their contribution to the message of the canon as a whole.[4]

In general, the method of interpretation one applies to the gospels has to be appropriate to the purpose for which one is reading them. Historical aims require the application of historical methods, literary readings require the application of literary criticism, sociological study requires the application of models from the social sciences, and so on. The aim of this study is to describe and evaluate the spirituality of the gospels in their canonical context. Such a task is necessarily multifaceted. It therefore requires the use of a variety of methods and approaches—part historical, part literary, part sociological, part theological. Furthermore, while I am concerned in what follows to describe as accurately as possible how the four evangelists envisage life lived in response to the revelation of God-in-Christ, I am concerned also to evaluate it. For the Christian theologian, the tasks of description and evaluation go together. Otherwise it is not possible to appropriate the message of the gospels in a life-giving way for the church in each succeeding generation. Placing ourselves 'under' scripture is not the same as enslaving ourselves to it.

There is, in my view, good reason for an attempt to give an account of the spirituality of the gospels. First, the burgeoning literature on spirituality in general and on Christian spirituality in particular is testimony to the fact that spirituality is on the agenda, both at the popular and the scholarly levels.[5] The roots of this interest are complex. Factors of obvious relevance include: the continued questioning of the cult of enterprise and materialism in the West; the collapse of Marxist ideology in the East and the accompanying resurgence of Orthodox and Roman Catholic Christianity; dialogue and conflict between adherents of the world religions in multi-cultural societies; concerns about the environment, leading to the quest for more ecologically aware ways of being human; trends in popular culture, such as new religious movements, the 'new age' movement, and the like; and in the churches, the reawakening of interest in traditional spiritualities, the impact of the charismatic movement, the cry of the oppressed for a spirituality of liberation, and the quest for a feminist spirituality promoted by the women's movement. A study of the spirituality of the gospels is timely, therefore, in view of this very widespread resurgence of interest in spirituality generally.

Second, surprisingly little has been written so far on the spirituality of the gospels, either taking each gospel as a unified whole or taking the gospels together in their contribution to the canon of scripture.[6] In historical-critical study of the gospels, the tendency is to break the text down into its constituent parts; and enormous energy is devoted to tracing the history of the formation of the tradition from its origins at the (hypothetical) oral stage to its final form as written text. This is valuable work, for it helps us to discern what the text means against the backdrop of the developments through which it may have passed. Unfortunately, however, there is a tendency for the meaning of the text as a whole in its final form to be lost sight of, and for the agenda of the historian to displace the theological and ethical concerns of the text itself or the concerns of the community of believers who hold the text as sacred scripture. On the other hand, within the churches, the common approach to the gospels in the quest for inspiration and guidance is to look for the 'purple passages' which speak with an apparent immediacy and vitality, the result of which is, once again, to fragment the gospel texts in a way which so easily loses sight of the larger whole. This tendency is exacerbated by common liturgical practice, where choices for the lectionary appear often to run counter to the natural shape of the biblical texts themselves.

A third reason for writing a book on the spirituality of the gospels is more personal. For four years I taught biblical studies at a theological college. My students were ordinands for ministry in the Church of England. Their goal was spiritual and ministerial formation within the Christian, and specifically, Anglican traditions. As a result, as one trained in the academic study of the Bible, I found myself being encouraged constantly to ask the question, how does this or that way of reading the text convey a sense of God, illumine the way ahead, inspire for the journey of faith, address the mission of the church in the world? If the Bible is a kind of 'love letter from God', as Christians believe, how best may we open it and be captivated by this text and its 'author'? In being encouraged to ask these questions on behalf of others, I came to ask them for myself. The 'quest of the historical Jesus' still excited me, questions about authorship and

5

dating and place of writing remained important, debates over whether or not Jesus (or Moses or Paul) *in fact* did or said this or that, continued to engage my attention. At the same time, however, I came to ask more urgently and more personally, how may I so read the text that it becomes for me—for us—what has always been claimed for it: that it is *Christian scripture*, a fount and wellspring of truth for people of faith who long to know God and to do God's will in the world? To put it another way, how may my/our reading of the text become a coherent and integral part of the worship of God in all of life? It is questions such as these which have led me to ask after the spirituality of the gospels, in the belief that the gospels are works of spirituality themselves and may appropriately be read as foundations of and for Christian spirituality today.

It has occurred to me more than once in the writing of this book that I am not the best person to be doing it. I say this not from false modesty, but from an awareness that spirituality and the study of spirituality are inevitably self-involving,[7] and therefore, that the best spirituality is likely to be written by one who has progressed in the life of the spirit and life in the Spirit. Saint Paul put it this way: 'The unspiritual person does not receive the gifts of the Spirit of God, for they are folly to him, and he is not able to understand them because they are spiritually discerned. The spiritual person judges all things, but is himself to be judged by no one' (1 Cor. 2.14–15). For one reason or another—to do, no doubt, with factors of cultural background, education, upbringing, religious subculture, habits of mind, emotion and will, and so on—the reading of the gospels I give will be myopic at some points and blind at others. All I can do here is to acknowledge this fact and to try to incorporate an awareness of it into what I write.

Notes

1.   This is not an idiosyncratic definition by any means. For example, Gordon S. Wakefield, in his excellent essay on 'Spirituality' in *idem*, ed., *A Dictionary of Spirituality* (London: SCM Press, 1983), pp. 361–3, defines it thus: 'This is a word which has come into vogue to describe those attitudes, beliefs, practices which animate people's lives and help them to reach out towards super-sensible realities.' And, speaking specifically of Christian spirituality, he says: 'Mutual

INTRODUCTION

indwelling with God in Christ is at once the means and the end; but this is a being caught up into the paschal mystery, not absorption into the infinite, and it cannot deliver us from the sometimes unbearable tensions, dangers and sufferings of "the world of action"'. Cf. also C. Garner's essay, 'What on Earth is Spirituality?', in J. Robson and D. Lonsdale, eds., *Can Spirituality Be Taught?* (London: ACATE and BCC, no date), pp. 1–8.

2. For a good recent account, see G.N. Stanton, *The Gospels and Jesus* (Oxford: Oxford University Press, 1989). Part I is entitled, 'The Four Gospels', and the headings for each respective gospel are suggestive for spirituality—for Mark the heading is 'The Way of Jesus', for Matthew it is 'The Way of Righteousness', for Luke it is 'God's Way Triumphs', and for John it is 'I am the Way'.

3. See further, R.A. Culpepper, 'Story and History in the Gospels', *Review & Expositor*, 81 (1984), pp. 467–78; also R. Morgan with J. Barton, *Biblical Interpretation* (Oxford: Oxford University Press, 1988), chs.6–8; and, as one attempt, P. Grant, *Reading the New Testament* (London: Macmillan, 1989).

4. The major contributor here is Brevard S. Childs, *The New Testament as Canon: An Introduction* (London: SCM Press, 1984).

5. See, for example, these three recent, substantial dictionaries/encyclopedias: G.S. Wakefield, ed., *A Dictionary of Christian Spirituality* (London: SCM Press, 1983); C. Jones, G. Wainwright, E. Yarnold, eds., *The Study of Spirituality* (London: SPCK, 1986); and E. Cousins, ed., *World Spirituality: An Encyclopedic History of the Religious Quest* (New York: Crossroad, 1985ff.; and London: SCM Press, 1989ff.), which includes three volumes on Christian spirituality. A useful survey article is G.S. Wakefield, 'Recent Books on Spirituality and their Trends', *Epworth Review*, 14/3 (1987), pp. 92–7.

6. To take a few examples, Gordon Mursell's excellent book *Out of the Deep: Prayer as Protest* (London: Darton, Longman & Todd, 1989) devotes its first four chapters to the biblical literature, but the texts chosen are primarily from the Old Testament, and Jesus and the gospels come in for attention only in relation to Gethsemane and Golgotha, in a brief section on pp. 22–5. Similarly, Rowan Williams' recently republished, *The Wound of Knowledge: Christian Spirituality from the New Testament to St John of the Cross* (London: Darton, Longman & Todd, 1990[2]) covers the New Testament suggestively, but only briefly, on pp. 4–14. C.P.M. Jones has a chapter on the New Testament in *The Study of Spirituality* (see note 5), pp. 58–89, but his discussion of the Synoptic Gospels is really about Jesus rather than about the spirituality of the gospels themselves, and his discussion of the Fourth Gospel is more a summary of scholarly findings about its message than an analysis of its spirituality. Closer to what I have done is Michael T. Winstanley's *Come and See: An*

7

Exploration into Christian Discipleship (London: Darton, Longman & Todd, 1985), but whereas he works synthetically, drawing upon material from all four gospels to address a particular theme, I take the four gospels one by one and only then try to draw together some common threads. Very suggestive for spirituality is J.L. Houlden's short study, *Backward into Light: The Passion and Resurrection of Jesus according to Matthew and Mark* (London: SCM Press, 1987), from which I have learnt much and try here to take further in relation to all four gospels.

7. Cf. Anthony de Mello, *The Song of the Bird* (Gujarat: Anand Press, 1982), pp. 12–13, on True Spirituality: 'The Master was asked, "What is Spirituality?" He said, "Spirituality is that which succeeds in bringing one to Inner Transformation."'

1

'You therefore must be perfect, as your heavenly Father is perfect'

THE SPIRITUALITY OF MATTHEW

Introduction

The Gospel of Matthew opens with a lengthy and seemingly contrived genealogy, beginning with Abraham and descending in a patriliny of three groups of fourteen names down to Jesus (Matt. 1.2–17). To most readers today, this hardly makes engrossing reading, and in church lectionaries Matthew's genealogy does not bulk large. Far preferable, it would seem, the gusto of the beginning of Mark or the air of orderly piety pervading the two linked birth stories at the beginning of Luke or the sonorous, measured poetry of the Prologue of John. If Matthew is a work of spirituality, its point of departure is not very promising. Leave that bit to the antiquarians!

Or are appearances deceptive? If we persevere, a reward is in store. Something subversive is going on. Matthew's genealogy can properly be called a 'subversive genealogy'.[1] First, it is as if creation is starting all over again. This is implied by the heading which opens the gospel and precedes the genealogy (cf. 1.1). The first two words, *biblos geneseos*—literally, 'book of genesis'—take us back to the book of Genesis at the beginning of the Bible. There, not only is *Genesis* the name of the Greek version of the book, but the very words *biblos geneseos* are used in connection with the story of creation and the story of Adam (cf. LXX Gen. 2.4; 5.1). It is as if Matthew is writing the story of Jesus as a counterpart to the story of Genesis. Moses' story of creation is being recast in terms of Matthew's story of new creation, something which other early Christian writers like Paul and John do in different ways also (cf. 1 Cor. 15.42–50; John 1.1–18). So the genealogy of Jesus proclaims a new beginning in the history of humankind and of the whole created order.

Second, the history of God's chosen people Israel is being

rewritten: 'So all the generations from Abraham to David were fourteen generations, and from David to the deportation to Babylon fourteen generations, and from the deportation to Babylon to the Christ fourteen generations' (1.17). This is no pedantic repetition of names and numbers for the sake of dull readers. Rather, it represents a bold claim that Israel's history is under God's careful control and that the successive periods of patriarchs, monarchy, and exile have reached their point of fulfilment in the birth of the messiah. This is the long-awaited Davidic messiah: for the number fourteen is the numerical value of the letters of the name 'David' in Hebrew. So Jesus is the Davidic king—and triply so! No wonder Herod took such desperate measures to nip in the bud the rule of one who, unlike himself, qualified by birth for kingship in Israel. The birth of the Davidic messiah presaged the death of the old order and the overthrow of all associated with it.

As a final point—although much more could be said[2]—the genealogy anticipates what comes later in the gospel and what the gospel as a whole is trying to say. Thus, the list of names foreshadows the most important naming of all, which takes place when Jesus himself is born (cf. 1.21, 23, 25). Also, the four women in the genealogy foreshadow the role of Mary in the messiah's birth. The fact that they are all Gentiles (or have a Gentile connection) may anticipate the inclusion of Gentiles in the people of God which the birth of the messiah makes possible. Not only a new king, therefore, but a new people also.

These few comments on Matthew's genealogy are meant to show that there is more to Matthew than meets the eye. Even a prosaic-looking list of names turns out to be subversive and epoch-making. For names have to do with identity and belonging, and lists of names are used to legitimate kings. The king of whom Matthew's gospel speaks is Jesus. The kingdom into which he invites his readers is the kingdom of heaven. Matthean spirituality springs out of encounter with that king and involves entry into that kingdom. It is appropriate now to trace the contours of this spirituality in more detail.

Matthean spirituality described

1. What is of the essence of Christian spirituality? Fundamentally, it is *a sense of the divine presence*: for Christian spirituality

has to do with the experience of that presence and living in the light of it. Matthew's way of putting this would be to say that Christian spirituality is based on the sure experience of the fatherly grace of God by which it is possible to say, in response, 'Our Father' (6.9). For Matthew, the starting point for spirituality is certainly the sense of the presence of God. He makes this plain in the way he tells the story of the life of Jesus.

First, the beginning of his Gospel emphasizes the divine presence. The orderly genealogy shows God's sovereignty over history, preparing the way for the birth of the Messiah (1.2–17), as we have seen. The conception of Jesus is thoroughly miraculous and is attributed to the work of the Holy Spirit (1.18, 20). Most importantly, the names given to the one who is to be born bear witness to the divine presence and to divine grace: 'You shall call his name Jesus, *for he will save his people from their sins*' (1.21); and, 'his name shall be called Emmanuel (*which means, God with us*)' (1.23). So, for Matthew, Jesus is God with us and God's divine agent of salvation.[3]

It is hardly coincidental that the end of Matthew's gospel emphasizes the divine presence as well. The events accompanying and following Jesus' death have the quality of a theophany (27.51ff.): the tearing, from top to bottom, of the temple curtain; the earthquake; the miraculous opening of the tombs and the resurrection of the saints; the awe-struck confession of the centurion; a second earthquake, this time at the tomb of Jesus; the angelic appearance to the women; and the appearances of the risen Jesus himself, first to the women, and then to the eleven. If, in his birth, Jesus is 'God with us' as saviour, so too, his death and resurrection manifest the divine, saving presence as well. Not only so. As Jesus' final words make plain, this presence is not restricted to these wondrous, past events. It is promised to followers of Jesus for all time: "Lo, I am with you always, to the close of the age' (28.20).

Between the beginning and the end of Matthew's story of Jesus, the sense of the divine presence (above all, in Jesus himself) is very strong also. The message which both John the Baptist and Jesus proclaim (in 3.2 and 4.17, respectively) is of the nearness of the coming of God: 'The kingdom of heaven is at hand'. At Jesus' baptism, the Spirit of God descends and 'alights' (Matthew only) on him, and the heavenly voice announces that he is God's 'beloved Son' (3.16–17). After this divine empowering, it is the Spirit who leads Jesus into the desert to be tested by the devil; and Jesus' steadfastness against the demonic shows that the presence of the divine has remained with him (4.1–11). As God's Son and Israel's Messiah, Jesus teaches with heavenly authority what is the will of God (e.g. chs. 5–7) and performs many miracles (e.g. chs. 8–9). He sends the disciples on mission and assures them of the Spirit's presence with them: 'It is not you who speak, but the Spirit of your Father speaking through you' (10.20). In prayer, Jesus addresses God in an intimate way as his Father and speaks of the unique revelation which the Father gives to him as the Son and the one who mediates knowledge of the Father to humankind (11.25–30). Finally, mention must be made of the transfiguration, in 17.1–8. This is another episode redolent of the divine presence: a bright cloud overshadows them on a high mountain (reminiscent of Sinai),[4] the heavenly voice speaks as at the baptism, and the disciples fall on their faces in homage and awe.

There are very strong grounds, therefore, for saying that, for the gospel of Matthew, spirituality begins (and ends) with the sense of the divine presence, and that Christian spirituality is a response to the presence of the divine *in Jesus*: for it is Jesus who is 'God with us' and who has promised to be with us always. So Matthew's spirituality is at one and the same time both *theocentric* and *christocentric*, a simultaneous focus of devotion given primary expression in the identification of God as the heavenly Father and Jesus as the divine Son.

2. This brings us to a second fundamental aspect of Matthean spirituality. If spirituality is grounded in a sense of the divine presence, how is that presence understood or experienced? For Matthew, *God's presence is experienced as fatherly*.[5] This has a number of dimensions.

First, it expresses *a belief in the providence of God*. As creator and sustainer of the world, God's providential care is for all created things. It is the heavenly Father who 'makes his sun rise on the evil and on the good, and sends rain on the just and on the unjust' (5.45). But this general providential care has a more intensive aspect as well. For God loves especially those who are his children and will not allow anything to befall them that is not within his will: 'Are not two sparrows sold for a penny? And not one of them will fall to the ground without your Father's will. But even the hairs of your head are all numbered' (10.29–30). The hyperbole captures beautifully a sense of the meticulous and scrupulous care of God for those who are his. The context of this saying in the discourse on mission shows that it is Christian missionaries who are in mind primarily, but there is no reason to think that what Jesus says to encourage them is not relevant also to believers in general.

Second, the sense of God as 'father' expresses *a recognition of the final authority of God and the appropriateness of humble dependence upon him*. Jesus shows this at the temptation (4.1–11). Tempted by one who would usurp God's place to become a usurper himself, Jesus resists. By showing his loyalty to the will of God and by refusing to contravene the word of God, Jesus shows himself to be *the* Son of the heavenly Father. The prayer which Jesus the Son teaches his disciples corresponds with this completely (6.9–13). It is a prayer to God as 'our Father', whose ultimate authority derives from the fact that he reigns 'in heaven'. The two halves of the prayer express well the two aspects of the divine fatherhood which we are talking about. The three 'thou' petitions come first and acknowledge the sovereignty of God. They are followed by the three 'we' petitions which express utter dependence on God for sustenance both material and spiritual.

Third, and to make explicit what is implicit in what has just been said, the experience of God as 'father' involves *an awareness of living in a spiritual relationship*. Once again, this involves a number of things. In positive terms, it involves a life of obedience to God and humility in the service of God, since, of course, the relationship is not a relationship between equals: the kingdom of heaven is utterly transcendent. The relationship is one of deep reciprocity, but it is a reciprocity between the One who dwells in heaven and his creatures who dwell on earth. This reciprocity comes to the fore in Matthew's doctrine of reward and punishment. In the teaching about forgiveness, at the end of the Lord's Prayer, for example, Jesus says: 'For if you forgive men their trespasses, your heavenly Father also will forgive you; but if you do not forgive men their trespasses, neither will your Father forgive your trespasses' (6.14–15). In negative terms, living in this spiritual relationship involves rejecting the temptation to behave autonomously or under the command of anyone other than God. Jesus expresses this supremely well. When, in the last temptation, the devil offers him all the kingdoms of the world in return for his obeisance, Jesus responds, 'Begone, Satan! for it is written, "You shall worship the Lord your God and him only shall you serve"' (4.10).

3. If spirituality in Matthew is a response to the sense of the fatherly presence of God and involves living in a spiritual relationship with God, it is important to try to specify *how that relationship is begun and maintained*. This takes us to the very heart of Matthew's writing and his understanding of Jesus and discipleship.[6]

The first thing to say is that, for Matthew, life with God and under God is something which is *initiated and sustained by God*. This is evident in the following. It is God who is 'with us' in Jesus, both at the beginning of the gospel and at its end, as we have seen already. The numerous 'formula quotations' (of the form, 'All this took place to fulfil what the Lord had spoken by the prophet . . .') show that it is the promises of God in scripture which are fulfilled in the story of Jesus. The message which both John and Jesus proclaim is of the coming of 'the kingdom *of heaven*', which is a periphrasis for the coming of God. And throughout the Gospel, it is God's divine agent, his Son Jesus, who pronounces blessings (5.3ff.), reveals the divine will (11.25–30), performs acts of healing with divine authority, casts out demons 'by the Spirit of God' (12.28), pronounces words of judgment (12.34ff.; 23.13–39), acknowledges his own divinity (16.17), founds the Church (16.18), gives his life in death 'for the forgiveness of sins' (26.28, Matthew only), and, after the resurrection, inaugurates and authorizes the mission to all nations (28.18–20). We are left in no doubt, then, that while (as we shall see) there is a strong emphasis on obedience and good works in Matthean spirituality, this occurs within a narrative theology which emphasizes even more, and first of all, *the saving grace of God*. It is not at all coincidental that Jesus' first great public discourse, the sermon on the mount, begins by pronouncing as blessed (by God) those who have only their spiritual poverty to offer (5.3).

But Matthew's gospel is at the same time *a summons to respond* to the divine grace revealed in and by Jesus. This response is characterized in many ways: repentance (3.2; 4.17); following Jesus (4.18–22; 8.18–22; 16.24); becoming 'poor in spirit' (5.3); demonstrating a 'righteousness (which) exceeds that of the scribes and Pharisees' (5.20); choosing the narrow gate and the hard way (7.13, 14); doing the will of the heavenly Father (7.21); having faith (8.10, 13; 9.2, 22, 29); hearing the word and understanding it (13.23); becoming like a child (18.3); being 'discipled' (28.19); and so on. If we can generalize on the basis of this great plethora of concepts and metaphors, we might say that the emphasis is, first, on the *spiritual* nature of the response—it concerns entry into the 'kingdom of heaven'; second, on the personal nature of the response—it is a response to God and to Jesus; and third, on the *wholehearted* nature of the response—as with the merchant who sells everything for the 'one pearl of great value' (13.46). It is clear as well that the way you begin is the way you continue: faith is required always, as Peter discovers to his cost in the episode of the walking on the water (14.28–33).

This spirituality is something which is *learned*. That is the next important point. Notice how this affects the portrayal of Jesus. Matthew presents Jesus as the Wisdom of God who teaches the will of God and summons people to listen and learn: '. . . Take my yoke upon you, and learn from me; for I am gentle and lowly in heart, and you will find rest for your souls. For my yoke is easy, and my burden is light' (11.29–30; cf. 13.54).[7] When a summary of Jesus' activity is offered, pre-eminence is given to Jesus' teaching (e.g. 4.23—'teaching in their synagogues . . .', Matthew only; cf. 9.35). Unlike the other gospels, Matthew organizes the sayings tradition into five major discourses in a way which highlights both Jesus' teaching role and the content of the teaching. Typically, Jesus chooses a location appropriate for the giving of revelation, and adopts the posture and role of the teacher, as at the beginning of the sermon on the mount: 'Seeing the crowds, he went up on the mountain, and when he sat down his disciples came to him. And he opened his mouth and taught them . . .' (5.1–2; cf. 13.1–2; 24.3). Typically also, each discourse ends in a formulaic way which draws attention to the didactic character of Jesus' activity: 'And when Jesus had finished these

15

sayings, the crowds were astonished at his teaching, for he taught them as one who had authority . . .' (7.28–29; cf. 11.1; 13.53; 19.1; 26.1). Matthew also has Jesus emphasize that he alone is to be recognized as 'teacher' (23.8).

Matthew's portrayal of the disciples also shows that this spirituality is something which is learned. When they are called, they follow the one who engages immediately in a ministry of teaching, preaching and healing (4.23), so they themselves are taught. The major discourses are directed primarily at them: '. . . and when he sat down his disciples came to him. And . . . he taught them . . .' (5.1–2; cf. 10.1ff.; 11.1; 13.10ff., 36ff.; 18.1; 23.1; 24.1; 26.1). It is as if the gospel as a whole is a kind of 'manual of instruction' for disciples of Jesus.[8] If you want to know how to qualify for entry into the kingdom of heaven, read the sermon on the mount (chs. 5–7). If you want to know how to engage in mission on behalf of the kingdom, read the mission instructions (ch. 10). If you want to know what the kingdom of heaven is like, read the parables of the kingdom (ch. 13). If you want help in matters of church order, read the manual of discipline (ch. 18). If you want teaching about the coming of the kingdom and how to be prepared, read the eschatological discourse at the end (chs. 23–25).

Not only is the gospel like a manual of instruction: the disciples turn out to be trained instructors![9] Thus, it is very noticeable that, in contrast to Mark, where the disciples are persistently obtuse and uncomprehending, the disciples in Matthew are able (somewhat imperfectly) to understand the teaching of Jesus. They are even likened to scribes, so concerned is Matthew to emphasize the scholarly, learned aspect of Christian spirituality. In material unique to Matthew, at the end of the parables of the kingdom, Jesus says to the disciples: '"Have you understood all this?" They said to him, "Yes". And he said to them, "Therefore every scribe who has been trained for the kingdom of heaven is like a householder who brings out of his treasure what is new and what is old."' To cap it all, in the great commission with which the gospel ends, the mission which is entrusted to the disciples is a mission of teaching: '. . . teaching them to observe all that I have commanded you' (28.20). We are left with the clear sense that they will be able to fulfil this commission, both because they have been taught by none other than the Son of God, and because they have been able learners.[10]

But if, according to Matthew, spirituality is something which is learned, it is important to ask, *how is it learned*? Is it learned by withdrawing into a monastic community to study Torah, as with the Covenanters at Qumran? Is it learned by going into the desert and sitting at the feet of an ascetic master, as Josephus did? Is it learned by attaching oneself to those zealots for the law, the Pharisees, of whom Saul who became Paul was one? Is it learned by conversion to philosophy and joining the retinue of a philosopher of Cynic, Stoic or Epicurean persuasion?[11] These are useful analogies: but none fits completely with Matthew.

For Matthew, the first and primary answer is that Christian spirituality is learned by *being with Jesus*. Note how Matthew highlights this idea. It comes in the naming of Jesus as 'Emmanuel', in 1.23. It comes as the final promise of the risen Jesus to the disciples, in 28.20. It comes as a promise to the church, in 18.20. And it comes in Matthew's editing of Mark's narrative: for example, in the story of Jesus in Gethsemane, where the disciples are told twice to '. . . watch *with me*' (26.38, 40; Matthew only). In the pre-Easter period, being with Jesus meant literally following him,[12] seeing his example and hearing his teaching. The absolute priority accorded such action finds expression in the subordination of otherwise legitimate ties and responsibilities: 'Another of the disciples said to him, "Lord, let me first go and bury my father." But Jesus said to him, "Follow me, and leave the dead to bury their own dead." And when he got into the boat, his disciples followed him.' (8.21–23). In the post-Easter period, being with Jesus becomes a matter of following his teaching, and participating in the life and mission of the new covenant people to whom he has given the promise of his spiritual presence: 'For where two or three are gathered in my name, there am I in the midst of them' (18.20).

Matthew's second, and closely related, answer is that Christian spirituality is learned by *hearing the commandments of Jesus* (as recorded in the gospel itself) *and doing them*. Not by coincidence does the sermon on the mount end with the parable of the wise and foolish builders (7.24–7). Here, the wise man is the one who 'hears these words of mine *and does them*', while the foolish man is the one who 'hears these words of mine *and does not do them*'.

17

The emphasis on learning through concrete acts of obedience is unmistakable. The sense of God's presence and providence comes in the asking, the seeking and the knocking (7.7–11). The discovery of Jesus' calming presence in stormy times comes only by following wherever he leads (8.23–7). The experience of the Father's Spirit speaking through the believer comes only when he or she obeys the call to go out on mission 'as sheep in the midst of wolves' (10.16ff.). In the terms of the dramatic story of Peter, in 14.28–33, it is only when Peter responds, however inadequately, to the command of Jesus to 'Come', that he receives divine power and experiences a miraculous salvation.

4. I have suggested that spirituality, according to Matthew, is something which is learned by being with Jesus, hearing his commandments, and doing them. It is appropriate now to elucidate *the kind of spiritual formation which the Jesus of Matthew demands*.[13]

First, there can be no doubt that Jesus demands *singleminded commitment*. It is this quality of commitment which Jesus practises himself. When tempted to transfer his allegiance to the devil, he cites from the Shema, the great summons of Torah to worship and serve the Lord alone (4.10; cf. Deut. 6.4ff.). When rebuked by Peter, having foretold his coming death and resurrection, Jesus responds with a severity arising out of total commitment to God: 'Get behind me, Satan! You are a stumbling-block (*skandalon*—Matthew only) to me, for you do not think the things of God, but the things of men' (16.22–23). When faced with the awful prospect of imminent arrest, trial and death, he affirms three times, in the very words he has taught his disciples to pray, his willingness to obey his heavenly Father's will: 'thy will be done' (26.36ff.).

As for Jesus, so also for his followers. The choice which he places before them is a choice between two incompatible ways which allows of no compromise. It is a matter of *either/or*: God or mammon (6.24); the narrow gate and the hard way or the wide gate and the easy way (7.13–14); building on the rock or building on the sand (7.24–7); being with Jesus or against him (12.30); making the tree and its fruit good or making them bad (12.33); being found at the last day to be a wise virgin or a foolish one, a faithful servant or an unfaithful one, amongst the sheep rather than amongst the goats (ch. 25). When the man comes to Jesus for instruction on the good thing he must do to gain eternal life, the Jesus of Matthew replies, 'If you would be perfect (*teleios*), go, sell what you possess, and give to the poor . . . and come, follow me', an action which the man's attachment to mammon prevents him doing (19.16–22). And when a Pharisee asks Jesus which is the great commandment of the law, he replies (once more drawing upon the Shema) with the double-command of love of God and love of neighbour (22.34–40). Nothing less than wholehearted, singleminded commitment to God and to the neighbour is the paradoxically easy yoke and light burden which the follower of Jesus is called to bear.

This demand for singleminded commitment has *an ascetic dimension* as well.[14] For example, the ability to control bodily needs and desires is given some emphasis. Fasting is one aspect of this. It is the practice of Jesus as he tests out his vocation in the wilderness: 'And he fasted forty days and forty nights, and afterward he was hungry' (4.2).[15] Unlike the Israel of old, which tested God by demanding food in the wilderness, Jesus, the embodiment of the true Israel, shows that feeding on the word of God is what is necessary (4.3–4). Interestingly, and according to the principle that what is good for the master is good for his followers, only the Jesus of Matthew offers detailed instruction on fasting, in the sermon on the mount (6.16–18; cf. also 9.14–15 par. Mark 2.18–20, noting especially Matthew's, 'Can the wedding guests *mourn* as long as the bridegroom is with them?'); and, typically, the accent is on fasting as a private discipline, alongside almsgiving and prayer (cf. 6.1–15). The asceticism is not extreme or total, however. Matthew is not at all reluctant to pass on the tradition that 'the Son of man came eating and drinking . . .' (11.19 par. Luke 7:34; cf. also Matt. 9.10–13). So it seems reasonable to conclude that there is a time and a place for ascetic discipline (cf. 9.15b; 26.29), but that doing the will of God does not require a commitment to an ascetic life *per se*.

Sexual control is another aspect of this singleminded commitment. Jesus himself does not marry; and he teaches strict sexual discipline. The prohibition of adultery and the extension of the prohibition to include lust, in the sermon on the mount (5.27–8), are without formal parallel in the synoptic tradition. Matthew emphasizes the need for strict control of bodily members by repeating the tradition about the eye and the hand which become causes of stumbling (5.29–30; 18.8–9); and he gives the tradition a specifically sexual connotation by setting it in the context of teaching about adultery (5.27–8). Even more noteworthy, however, is the teaching to the disciples alone, in 19.10–12, once again unique to Matthew. Here, in response to a disciple's comment on Jesus' strict prohibition of divorce and remarriage, that 'it is not expedient to marry', Jesus replies with a special word of revelation. It is the threefold saying about eunuchs, which climaxes with the words: '. . . and there are eunuchs who have made themselves eunuchs for the sake of the kingdom of heaven' (19.12). Matthew clearly allows for the possibility that devotion to the kingdom of heaven, especially commitment to mission (cf. 10.27–30 par. Mark 10.28–30), will involve for some the hard vocation to singleness and celibacy.[16]

A second aspect of the spiritual formation demanded by Jesus is *its stress on interiority and on what is hidden*, on the discipline and reshaping of the individual's will, emotions, allegiances and affections.[17] This is a natural complement to the concern for total commitment just mentioned, and it comes through in many ways. In the narrative as a whole, we find it in experiences of revelation and of the reception of the divine will secretly, through dreams, when appearances seem all to the contrary (e.g. 1.20; 2.12, 13, 19; cf. 27.19). In the portrayal of Jesus, we find it in the temptation, when Jesus rejects demands for public manifestations of power out of the prior consideration of inner, personal allegiance (4.1–11). In the teaching of Jesus, it is an all-pervasive element. One thinks, for example, of the blessing on 'the poor *in spirit*' (5.3); the antitheses substituting anger for murder (5.21–2) and the lustful look for the adulterous act (5.27–8); the teaching on works of piety, which stresses that almsgiving, praying and fasting be done in secret (6.1–18); the emphasis on the ethic of humility (5.5; 18.1–4); and the teaching on faith (e.g. 8.10, 26; 9.22, 29; 17.14–20). Most expressive is the searing attack on hypocrites and hypocrisy in chapter 23: 'Woe to you, scribes and Pharisees, hypocrites! for you cleanse the outside of the cup and of the plate, but inside they are full of extortion and rapacity. You blind Pharisee! first cleanse the inside of the cup and of the plate, that the outside also may be clean' (23.25–6; cf. 12.34–5; 15.1–20).

If we ask why Matthew places such stress on interiority as a fundamental aspect of spirituality, the answer may be that it is a way of drawing attention away from a spirituality of a different kind, one focussed more on ritual observances of one kind or another. For Matthew, what is of primary importance is right motivation and moral action. Ritual observances are of distinctly secondary importance: 'Woe to you, scribes and Pharisees, hypocrites! for you tithe mint and dill and cummin, and have neglected the weightier matters of the law, justice, mercy and faith; these you ought to have done, without neglecting the others' (23.23).

Another, equally significant, reason may be that the stress on interiority is a way of reinforcing the element of total demand in the teaching of Jesus: 'You, therefore, must be perfect (*teleioi*), as your heavenly Father is perfect (*teleios*)' (5.48). If true spirituality is a response to divine grace revealed in and by Jesus, as I suggested earlier, then it may be important to show that this is not a matter of *cheap* grace, especially if the consensus about the place of the law in the life of faith since the coming of the messiah is taken for granted no longer. So, Matthew's claim on the heart, mind and will of the believer may be seen as an expression of the biblical idea of election that, 'to whom much is given, much is required' (cf. 18.23–35; 21.33–43; 22.11–14; 24.45–51; 25.14–30). According to this perspective, what people do *not* see—that is, what is seen and known by the Father in heaven alone—is just as important, if not more so, than what people *do* see (cf. 23.1–12, esp. vv.5–7).

A final reason for the stress on interiority may be the need to provide a balance to the very strong emphasis Matthew places on practical action. Or, to use a metaphor from the parable of the sower, the stress on purity of heart and singleness of will seeks to encourage growth of the spiritual roots necessary to sustain active growth in doing good (cf. 13.18–23). So, for instance, Jesus himself prepares for mission by withdrawing to a secret, desert place and fasting (4.1–2). Similarly, as the culmination of his mission draws near, he withdraws to Gethsemane to pray (26.36–46). This pattern is consistent with the curious fact that Matthew, in contrast to Mark, appears to restrict the mission of the apostles to one of preaching and healing but not of teaching (Mark 6.30; omitted in Matt.10.1–11.1), and keeps the sending out on a teaching mission until the end (28.18–20). This is because they are not able to teach others properly until they themselves have been grounded fully in the teaching of Jesus.[18]

A third major aspect of the spirituality demanded by Jesus is that it is *an active, practical spirituality.* If the life of faith requires an assault on the citadels of the heart and will so that they are made captive to the hidden and revealed will of the heavenly Father, it also requires that the purified heart and the instructed will make good works possible. To put it another way, religion and morality are integrally related in Matthew, as they are in the faith of Israel and of the Judaism of Matthew's day. God's grace in revelation and covenantal election brings with it the responsibility of active obedience by God's people to the divine will. This is no less true with the revelation of God's grace in Jesus ('God with us'), who gives a new and definitive interpretation of God's will as the basis for the embodiment of the kingdom of heaven on earth.

Pre-eminent in this context is Matthew's unrivalled emphasis on *the love commandment.*[19] If the fifth antithesis rescinds the *lex talionis* (or law of reciprocity) (5.38–42), the sixth and final antithesis commands love of enemies (5.43–8). In Matthew's version of the story of the rich man, the commandments which Jesus lists culminate with the love commandment, 'You shall love your neighbour as yourself' (19.19; Matthew only). Equally striking is Matthew's version of the question about the great commandment (Mark 12:28–34 par. Matt. 22.34–40). Among the changes Matthew has made to his Marcan source are the following. First, Matthew's version is considerably abbreviated and focuses on a confrontation with hostile Pharisees (vv. 35–6) over the essentials of the law. For the Jesus of Matthew, the double commandment to love is that upon which 'all the law and the prophets depend' (v. 40; Matthew only). Second, Matthew repeats the description, unique to him, of the love commandment as 'the great (*megale*) commandment' (vv. 36, 38; Matthew only). Third, only Matthew describes the command to 'love your neighbour as yourself' as being 'like (*homoia*)' the command to love God, thus bringing neighbourly love into very close association with love of God. It seems fair to say, then, that the double command to love God and neighbour expresses in a nutshell what practical spirituality is about according to Matthew. This corresponds, on the negative side, with a serious concern that, in the last days, the life of the people of God will be threatened by many people's love growing cold (24.12).

Alongside love, we must place *the ethic of forgiveness and reconciliation.* A catalogue of the important material reveals that this is the concern of the first antithesis (5.21–6); that Matthew ends his version of the Lord's Prayer with teaching on forgiveness, as an elaboration of the second 'we-petition' (6.14–15; cf. v. 12); that according to 9.8 (diff. Mark 2.12), the authority to forgive sins has been given to ordinary mortals; and that Peter, the rock on which the church is to be built (16.18), is given specific and extended instruction on the obligation to forgive the erring brother 'seventy times seven' (18.21–35).[20]

Next, we should draw attention to what Matthew calls '*the weightier matters of the law*' (23.23).[21] Matthew clearly discriminates between one kind of law and another, and this is what we would expect, given his emphasis on the love command and on reconciliation, and given also what we described earlier as his stress on interiority. Broadly speaking, priority is given to moral concerns over ritual concerns (cf. 15.1–20). The 'weightier matters' in 23.23 are justice, mercy and faith. Focusing just on *mercy*, we note the following. The fifth beatitude proclaims a blessing upon those who show mercy (5.7). Jesus, the Son of David, shows mercy himself when he heals the blind men (9.27–30; 20.29–34), the Canaanite woman's daughter (15.21–28), and the epileptic boy (17.14–18). The parable of the unforgiving servant, unique to Matthew (18.23–35), reaches its climax with the words of the master to the servant: '. . . should not you have had mercy on your fellow servant, as I had mercy on you?' (v. 33). Most striking, perhaps, is Matthew's insertion, on two occasions, into the tradition he received from Mark, of the text from Hosea 6:6, 'I desire mercy and not sacrifice'. On the first occasion, the call of Levi (Mark 2:13–17 par. Matt. 9.9–13), Jesus is cast as a teacher (Matt. 9.11) who instructs the hostile Pharisees thus: 'Go and learn what this means, "I desire mercy and not sacrifice"' (9.13). And in Matthew's version of the plucking ears of grain on the sabbath episode (Mark 2.23–28 par. Matt. 12.1–8), Matthew considerably expands the reply of Jesus in defence of the disciples, including, once more, the quotation from Hosea 6.6, and implying that this is a lesson from scripture which the Pharisees are unable to learn (12.7).

Matthew's understanding of *righteousness* (*dikaiosune*) is yet another aspect of his concern for an active, practical spirituality. It is a concept uniquely important to Matthew amongst the synoptics, occurring without parallels, in 3.15; 5.6, 10, 20; 6.1, 33; and 21.32. Its meaning is uniform, and has to do with 'moral conduct in accord with God's will'.[22] Thus, at the outset of his public ministry, Jesus agrees to be baptized by John in order 'to fulfil all righteousness' (3.15). His humble obedience, from the start, to the call of his heavenly Father is made clear in his willingness to accept John's baptism of repentance. Towards the end of his public ministry, when Jesus is teaching in the temple, he tells the parable of the two sons (21.28–32; Matthew only). Once again, John figures: this time, in the interpretation of the parable, as the one who 'came . . . in the way of righteousness'. In other words, John called upon people to repent and do the will of God (cf. 3.1–10), something which the (impure) tax collectors and harlots were willing to do, and the (pure) priests and elders of the people were not.

All the remaining five occurrences of 'righteousness' come in the sermon on the mount. So the teaching of the sermon expresses pre-eminently what 'righteousness' means. In the beatitudes, it is something to hunger and thirst for (5.6), and something—presumably behaviour of some kind—liable to attract persecution (5.10; cf. 23.34–5). In 5.17–20, the preamble to the teaching on how to interpret the law of Moses (5.21–48), the Jesus of Matthew defends his teaching against the charge of being antinomian and challenges his hearers to display a 'righteousness' greater than that of the scribes and Pharisees. This greater righteousness is spelt out in the so-called 'antitheses' which follow, each of which represents a more demanding interpretation of the Mosaic law. But the greater righteousness is also defined by what comes immediately before, in 5.19, where the emphasis is on *doing* the commandments, not just teaching them: 'But he who does them and teaches them shall be called great in the kingdom of heaven'. Righteousness according to Matthew is a matter, not just of knowing what is right, but of doing it as well.[23] This is confirmed by the other two occurrences of the term in the sermon. In introducing the next block of teaching, on almsgiving, prayer and fasting (6.2–18), Jesus warns, 'Beware of *doing your righteousness* before men in order to be seen by them . . .' (6.1).[24] Clearly, righteousness here is something very practical: it includes almsgiving, for example. Finally, in 6.33, Jesus teaches that daily material needs will be met by the heavenly Father if the disciple makes as his first priority the seeking after God's righteousness, that is, if he aligns his behaviour with the right conduct God requires.[25]

What is said about righteousness (*dikaiosune*) is reinforced by what is said about the righteous (*dikaios*) person. Joseph is described as *dikaios* (1.19), and this is seen in the fact that he does what God or the angelic messenger tells him to do (1.24; 2.13–15, 19–21, 22–3). Jesus, too, is described as *dikaios*, by Judas (27.4) and by Pilate's wife (27.19; Matthew only): so even his enemies recognize that he dies as the righteous servant of God. And there are several parables where a clear distinction is drawn between the righteous and the unrighteous, and each time the criterion for the division is whether or not God's will has been done. So, in the interpretation of the parable of the weeds (13.36–43), the righteous are separated from those who are designated, significantly, 'those committing lawlessness' (13.41, my trans.; cf. RSV, 'evil-doers'!). In the parable of the net (13.47–50), a sorting out takes place between those who are 'righteous' and those who are 'evil'. Above all, in the so-called parable of the sheep and the goats (25.31–46), the great separation which takes place is between the nations which have performed acts of mercy and hospitality towards itinerant missionaries and those nations which have not. The former, the ones who have engaged in acts of love of the neighbour and have fulfilled the law, therefore, are designated 'the righteous' (25.37, 46).

Another theme deserves attention because it also contributes to the absolute priority Matthew gives to the concrete, practical dimension of Christian spirituality. That is the theme of *bearing fruit*. It is a theme which Matthew inherits from the tradition: for example, the material he shares with Luke on the message of John the Baptist summoning Israel to 'bear fruit that befits repentance' (Matt. 3.7–10 par. Luke 3.7–9); and the material he shares with Mark on the cursing of the unfruitful fig tree (Mark 11.12–14 par. Matt. 21.18–19). But it is a theme which Matthew also develops further, so conducive is it to his purposes. Thus, in the sermon on the mount, Matthew takes over a traditional saying about bearing fruit in order to provide a criterion for distinguishing true and false prophets (Matt. 7.15–20 par. Luke 6.43–45); and he brackets the traditional material with the repeated warning, 'You will know them by their fruits' (7.17, 20). Especially significant are the modifications Matthew makes to the parable of the wicked tenants (Mark 12.1–12 par. Matt. 21.33–46). Whereas the focus of the parable in Mark is on the reprehensible behaviour of the tenants towards the vineyard owner and his envoys, the focus in Matthew's version is also on the failure of the tenants to produce a fruitful vineyard. Hence, 'He . . . will let out the vineyard to other tenants *who will give him the fruits in their seasons*', in v. 41 (italicized, Matthew only); and the entire concluding verse, which says, 'Therefore I tell you, the kingdom of God will be taken away from you and given to a nation producing the fruits of it' (v. 43, Matthew only). The significance of the Matthean modifications is that they draw attention to the responsibility of the elect people of God to demonstrate their elect status by being fruitful in good works. Failure to do so amounts to apostasy. This, according to Matthew, is the position of many in Israel (cf. v. 45). It is also a constant danger in the church: 'Not everyone who says to me, "Lord, Lord," shall enter the kingdom of heaven, but he who does the will of my Father who is in heaven' (7.21).

As an attempt to guard against apostasy of this kind, Matthew, more than any other gospel writer, warns of *the danger of being a 'hypocrite' (hupokrites)*, and typecasts the scribes and Pharisees as such. Hence, the vitriolic attack against them as 'hypocrites' in chapter 23 (cf. also 15.7; 22.18). From Matthew's use of *hupokrites* and *hypokrisis* ('hypocrisy'), it appears that a range of ideas is involved.[26] First, it means saying or believing one thing and doing another (or nothing at all): 'They preach but do not practise' (23.3). Note, in particular, the vivid depiction of the scribes and Pharisees as 'whitewashed tombs' (23.27), a metaphor which is then elaborated in terms which contrast an outward appearance of righteousness with an inward reality of 'hypocrisy *and lawlessness (anomia)*' (23.28), a juxtapostiton which shows that hypocrisy is regarded as a form of active disobedience to the will of God. Second, the hypocrite is one who does the right thing for the wrong reason, especially for the sake of appearances: 'They do all their deeds to be seen by men . . .' (23.5; cf. 6.2, 5, 16). Third, the hypocrite is one who lacks discernment, who is unable to distinguish what is fundamental in one's obligation to God and neighbour and what is peripheral. Witness the confrontation between Jesus and the scribes and Pharisees over the practice of the washing of hands (15.1–20), where Jesus controverts his opponents (as 'hypocrites', v. 7) and draws a clear distinction between the commandment (*entole*) of God and the tradition (*paradosis*) of the elders (v. 3), between the moral law and the ceremonial (vv. 4–6, 17–20). The hypocrite is a 'blind guide' (v. 14), totally unsuitable, therefore, to show the way to true obedience and right action.

If the kind of spirituality demanded by Jesus is an active, practical spirituality, it is by no means a 'lone ranger' spirituality. This is the final point that needs to be made before drawing our study of Matthew to a conclusion. The spirituality of Matthew is *a spirituality for the people of God*. This is implicit in what has been said already, but needs to be made explicit.

It is implicit, for instance, in what was said about the sense of God as Father: for the corollary of this is not only the christological one, that Jesus is the Son, but it is also the ecclesiological one, that followers of Jesus are *members of a spiritual household* (cf. 19.29).[27] To this end, Matthew places considerable emphasis on the idea of believers as a *brotherhood*. In the little 'manual of discipline' in chapter 18, the term used to refer to fellow members of the people of God, is 'brother' (*adelphos*), and great weight is placed on the obligation to practise an ethic of brotherly love and forgiveness (18.15ff., 21–2, 23–35—noting especially Matthew's allegorizing conclusion of the parable: 'So also my heavenly Father will do to every one of you, if you do not forgive *your brother* from your heart'). Furthermore, when Jesus teaches his disciples about authority relations, it is the familial model more than the school model which he commends : 'But you are not to be called rabbi, for you have one teacher, *and you are all brethren*' (23.8; Matthew only). So the spiritual life is a vocation to live in a relationship of humility, forgiveness and love with one's fellow-members in the spiritual family of God's people.

It is also a vocation to be *the church*.[28] Of all four evangelists, only Matthew uses the term *ekklesia*, so beloved of Paul, to describe the people of God (16.18; 18.17); and this signifies how important the corporate dimension of spirituality is for him. For the church replaces Israel as God's new people.[29] The story Matthew tells is of the coming of the messiah to Israel, the messiah's revelation of the true and demanding will of God, his founding of the church under the authority of Peter (16.18–19), his acceptance by a few and his rejection by the many in Israel, his death as an act of national apostasy (27.25; cf. 21.33–43), and his post-resurrection commission to the disciples to reconstitute the people of God by a mission to all nations. This means that Matthean spirituality involves *becoming and being the kind of people Israel was meant to be*: an elect people wholeheartedly devoted to the service of God as taught by God's messiah; a people of humble piety and fraternal love, noted for its ethic of forgiveness both to insiders and to outsiders; a people devoted both to the study of the scriptures and to obedience to its ordinances as interpreted by Jesus; and a people surpassing others in righteousness and, in consequence, shining out as 'the light of the world' (5.14). In short, the church is to be the embodiment and reflection of the coming kingdom of heaven, on earth in the here and now (cf. 5.48).

Conclusion

What I have said about the spirituality of the gospel of Matthew is by no means exhaustive, and hardly does justice to the nuances of the gospel as a whole. But in conclusion, I would like to present a few further reflections and critical observations in order to suggest, perhaps, where further thought might be given.

1. First, even though Matthew places great emphasis on spirituality as obedience to the will of God as taught by Jesus, it is crucial to draw a lesson from the gospel genre which Matthew has used, and to point out in consequence that Matthean spirituality is *story-shaped not Torah-shaped*. Matthew's gospel contains commandments and community rules, but it cannot be reduced to them. Rather, it is 'messianic biography',[30] and spirituality is a personal response—both at the individual and at the corporate levels—to that biography. Wayne Meeks puts

28

this well: 'Matthew makes that story part of the grammar of Christian ethics. The commandments are not separable from the commander, the teachings from the teacher. Discipleship is "following" the person identified in the story, who, raised from the dead, goes on leading the community.'[31]

A corollary of this is that there is a sense in which spirituality, according to Matthew, is not given. It remains *something to be worked out and to be worked at*. What *is* given is the story of the messiah and of the breaking into the present of the kingdom of heaven. The commandments contained in the story are hardly comprehensive: rather, they have a more exemplary quality, 'reminding the members of the community's intensive claims'.[32] Many things are left open to decisions and actions of the church and its leaders in the future. Hence, Peter is given the 'keys of the kingdom' (16.19), and the authority to 'bind' and 'loose' is given both to him and to the church (16.19; 18.18).

What is given also, and most importantly, is the promise of the ever-abiding presence of Jesus (28.20). But discerning that presence is not a matter immune from doubt. Even when the risen Lord appears to the Eleven, Matthew tells us that 'some doubted' (28.17). That is why faith, child-like humility, a spirit of generous forgiveness, and a reluctance to be judgmental are all necessary. It is why criteria for testing the words of prophets claiming to speak in the name of the Lord are needed, as well. Entering the narrow gate and going the hard way are ventures as fraught with difficulty and temptation for the follower of Jesus as they were for Jesus himself. Even with a gospel which attempts to provide more grounds for certainty than its predecessor (Mark), this remains the case.

2. If Matthew's vision of Christian spirituality is that it is a venture fraught with difficulty and temptation, it is fair to ask *whether Matthew's own 'spiritual exercise' in writing this Gospel has succumbed to temptations of any kind*? Is Matthew the best guide to what it means to 'follow' Jesus? The problems I have in mind include the following.

First, what are we to make of Matthew's *hostility to the Jews*? Only in Matthew is there the vitriolic attack on the scribes and Pharisees of chapter 23. Only Matthew has the whole Jewish people (*ho laos*) at the crucifixion cry out, 'His blood be on us

29

and on our children!' (27.25). Only Matthew has the legend of the bribing of the guards from the empty tomb by the chief priests and elders of the people (28.11–15). And all of this, what is more, in a gospel which places such emphasis on the love commandment, including the command to love your enemies! It would appear that the moral horizon of Matthew's gospel has become seriously clouded at this point. The gospel which says most about hypocrisy appears, on this issue, to have become itself most hypocritical. Historically, this may be explained quite plausibly as the result both of the persecution experienced by the Matthean followers of Jesus at the hands of their Jewish compatriots and of the intense rivalry which developed between church and synagogue in the period before and after the First Jewish War.[33] There can be little doubt also, that the kind of vituperative attack on the Pharisees attributed to Jesus in chapter 23 and elsewhere, owes much to rhetorical conventions of Matthew's day, conventions which he shared with his confreres in Judaism. Witness the language used of outsiders by the Qumran Covenanters, for instance.[34] However, neither of these arguments entirely relieves Matthew of the burden of the problem of his anti-Judaism. With the wisdom of hindsight, and particularly in the light of the Holocaust, we have to conclude that his own application of the love commandment was seriously and tragically blinkered.

Second, what are we to make of Matthew's *doctrine of reward and punishment*? There can be no doubt that such doctrine is all-pervasive in Matthew and that it is a constitutive part of his overall indebtedness to the world-view of traditional Jewish apocalyptic.[35] According to the Matthean doctrine, the kingdom of heaven is breaking in with the coming of the messiah and a great sorting out is about to take place on the basis of both Israel's and the nations' response to the revelation of the will of God by his Son Jesus. Those who respond by faith and good works will inherit the kingdom of heaven; those who harden their hearts and refuse to repent will be cast into 'the eternal fire prepared for the devil and his angels' (25.41). Examples of this apocalyptic dualism are numerous: the preaching of John the Baptist at the beginning of the gospel (3.7–12), the teaching of Jesus in the sermon on the mount (e.g. 5.22, 29, 30; 7.13–14, 24–7), the mission instructions (10.14–15, 32–3), the parables of the kingdom (e.g. 13.30, 36–43, 47–50), the teaching about causes of 'stumbling' in the manual of discipline (18.5–6, 7–9), the attack on the hypocrisy of the Pharisees (23.29–36), and the parables about the end time (e.g. the wedding banquet, in 22.1–14; the talents, in 25.14–30; and the sheep and the goats, in 25.31–46).

In the face of such material, it has seriously to be asked whether we do not have here an attempt at a kind of moral and religious bludgeoning: 'Do this, or else!' In a gospel so concerned with matters of the heart and the importance of right motivation, with the integrity of inner disposition and outward performance, are not promises of heavenly reward and threats of eternal damnation likely to *subvert* moral character in the direction of self-interest? And how are we to reconcile a doctrine of eternal punishment with this gospel's moral imperative of love of enemies, an imperative applicable, presumably, to God as judge, as well? Once again, it is possible to think of mitigating factors and extenuating circumstances which help to explain Matthew's doctrine. Thus, extreme problems inside the community, especially the possible threat to its life and mission posed by false prophets and antinomian charismatics (cf. 7.15–20, 21–3), may be said to justify extreme solutions, where moral niceties need to be set aside and replaced by something more blatant and even coercive.[36] Likewise, threats posed by the hostility and animosity of outsiders help to explain a doctrine of reward and punishment intended to bolster the identity and self-esteem of those so threatened. But understanding whence a doctrine originated and how it may have been intended to function in particular historical circumstances by no means *justifies* it as true. On the contrary, awareness of the historical conditioning of Matthean spirituality helps us to see that, in certain respects, Matthew's moral horizon was not only clouded, but limited as well.

A third critical reflection has to do with what has been called *Matthew's willingness to satisfy 'the insatiable demand to have all inquiries answered and faith provided with a water-tight case'*.[37] This is especially clear when Matthew is compared with Mark, his source, in order to see where Matthew has 'filled in the gaps' left by Mark or tidied up Mark's account. So, for example, in their respective resurrection accounts, where Mark ends in a

31

rather opaque and open-ended way, with no actual appearance of the risen Lord and the women fleeing from the empty tomb and saying nothing (Mark 16.1–8), Matthew provides two appearance stories, first to the women, who go and tell the disciples what they have heard and seen (28.8, 9–10, 11a, 16), and second to the disciples themselves (28.16–18). Where Mark leaves the women's question about the tombstone unanswered (Mark 16.3–4) and tells of the appearance to the women of a 'young man' (Mark 16:5), Matthew replaces the young man with an angel of the Lord who descends from heaven (to the accompaniment of a 'great earthquake'!), and says that it was the angel who rolled back the stone from the tomb (28.2). Where Mark's story leaves open (by not mentioning) the possibility that there might be another explanation of the empty tomb, Matthew takes the bull by the horns and tells two stories, the first showing that the body of Jesus could not have been stolen, since guards were stationed at the tomb (27.62–6), the second explaining how (by means of the bribing of the guards) the theory that Jesus' body had been stolen arose (28.11–15). In short, where Mark's account of the resurrection appears open-ended and shrouded in mystery, Matthew's appears literal, transparent and 'factual'.

Do changes of this kind—and many more could be noted—represent a kind of failure of nerve on Matthew's part? Do they lay bear a spirituality less profound, less mature, less open to risk and doubt, in comparison to the spirituality of the gospel of Mark? There is, I think, something in this. There is a clear tendency in Matthew to overcome doubt with evidences and authoritative teaching of one kind or another in order to provide a basis for greater certainty: certainty, where tentativeness and questioning faith may be more legitimate. Even where doubt is mentioned, as in the account of the final resurrection appearance to the Eleven (28:17), one suspects that it was too prominent an element in the pre-Matthean resurrection tradition for Matthew to omit it entirely (cf. Luke 24.13ff.; John 20.24–9; 1 Cor. 15; also Mark 8:31–3 and parallels); and one notices also what is so characteristic of Matthew, that the potentially problematic fact that 'some doubted' is resolved immediately and in no uncertain terms by the appearance of Jesus on the mountain with them and his authoritative declaration and commission, both designed to dispel all doubt.

Perhaps there is good reason for Matthew's stance. Perhaps for Matthew there was no point in making a virtue of doubt. Perhaps his pastoral instincts encouraged him to try to protect and bolster the weak and vulnerable faith of his community of believers in messiah Jesus when considerable pressure was coming from the Pharisaic apologists of formative Judaism to return to the fold of the synagogue. Perhaps he felt that the mission to all nations, Jews as well as Gentiles, made it imperative to foster a distinctively Christian apologetic, aimed at answering the objections of opponents and providing evidence for inquirers.[38] Be that as it may, the question remains to what extent Matthew's revision and interpretation of the tradition provide the basis for a mature, questioning, ecumenical spirituality, where what is important is discerning the mystery, not knock-down proofs.

3. One final reflection has to do with *the implications of Matthew's place in the canon* for understanding Matthean spirituality. This is a question rarely asked,[39] partly because some trends in scholarship have encouraged the analysis of one book of the Bible apart from, and even over against, another—and with very fruitful results, as I hope the preceding discussion shows. But there is something to be said also for reading each individual book within the context of its place in the book of scripture as a whole, not least because the Bible as a whole is the church's scripture, not just any one book within it. So: does it make any difference for Matthean spirituality to read Matthew as the first book of the New Testament, coming after the end of the Old Testament?

Certainly, it helps us to see that the spirituality of Matthew is *fundamentally biblical and traditional* in its shape and texture.[40] Its continuities with Old Testament spirituality are **very** strong. In both, gracious revelation and divine presence precede the enunciation of covenantal obligations. In both, an elect people is chosen to serve God as a light to the nations. In both, covenantal obligations are moral and cultic, and are intended to express and enable wholehearted devotion to the one, true God. In both, love of God and love of neighbour take priority in the life of faith. In both, God's 'son' is the agent of his saving purpose: Israel, in the Old Testament; Jesus, and the followers of Jesus, in Matthew. In both, the prospect is held out of the coming of God in judgment, to reward the righteous and to punish the disobedient. So we cannot really hope to make sense of Matthean spirituality on its own: for it is thoroughly indebted to its roots in the Bible and in Judaism. These strong continuities, this deep-rootedness, mean that the spirituality of Matthew has a pedigree. It has been tested and refined over time and in the lives of generations of people. This recognition helps to explain Matthew's 'conservatism' with respect to the tradition (e.g. 5.17–19; and note Matthew's omission of the Marcan editorial comment, 'Thus he declared all foods clean' (Mark 7.19b), at 13.16). He knows that, however much in need of reform and renewal in the light of new revelation, the tradition is too valuable to criticise freely or to dispense with at will. The wise householder brings out of his treasure, not just what is new, *but what is old, as well* (13.52).

But Matthew also stands at the beginning of the New Testament: so there is discontinuity with the tradition as well as continuity. The fulcrum of this discontinuity lies in the meaning given to the term 'son of God'. It is central to Matthew's concerns to show that *Jesus* is the Son of God,[41] and that God's promises to Israel (and through Israel to the nations) are fulfilled, completed and surpassed now in him, because Jesus is 'God with us'. So, for instance, the life of Jesus fulfils scripture (e.g. 1.23; 2.6, 15, 18, 23); the teaching Jesus gives is a deeper revelation of the will of God and the kingdom of heaven, and enables a greater righteousness; and the death of Jesus 'for the forgiveness of sins' inaugurates a new covenant (26.28).

This means that Matthean spirituality must be significantly different, in certain respects, from the spirituality of the Old Testament. One difference is that it is christocentric: it is about following Jesus, doing and teaching the commandments of Jesus, and responding to the presence of God in Jesus. Another difference is that it is eschatological: it is about living the life of the heavenly kingdom under the conviction that the kingdom of heaven has been inaugurated by Jesus' death and resurrection (cf. 27.51ff.). A final difference is that it is ecclesiological: it is about living as a member of the spiritual brotherhood of the church, the 'true Israel' founded by Jesus,[42] whose membership is open to people who have been 'discipled' from among all the nations. These are the householder's *new* treasures. In Matthew's view of things, they are of inestimable value. For these spiritual treasures, as for the pearl of great price (13.45–6), it is worth sacrificing everything.

Notes

1. I have borrowed the term from Judith N. Shklar, 'Subversive Genealogies', in C. Geertz, ed., *Myth, Symbol and Culture* (New York: Norton, 1971), pp. 129–154. On the functions of the gospel genealogies in comparative perspective, see R.T. Hood, 'The Genealogies of Jesus', in A. Wikgren, ed., *Early Christian Origins* (Chicago: Quadrangle, 1961), pp. 1–15.

2. The authoritative commentary is R.E. Brown, *The Birth of the Messiah* (London: Chapman, 1977); and see, most recently, the masterly ICC commentary by W.D. Davies and D.C. Allison, *The Gospel According to Saint Matthew*, vol. 1 (Edinburgh: T&T Clark, 1988).

3. On the importance of names and naming in Matthew's beginning, see K. Stendahl, '*Quis et Unde?* An Analysis of Matthew 1–2', in G.N. Stanton, ed., *The Interpretation of Matthew* (London: SPCK, 1983), pp. 56–66.

4. On the symbolic significance of the mountain in Matthew, see T.L. Donaldson, *Jesus on the Mountain: A Study in Matthean Theology* (Sheffield: JSOT, 1985).

5. Cf. H.F.D. Sparks, 'The Doctrine of the Divine Fatherhood in the Gospels', in D.E. Nineham, ed., *Studies in the Gospels: Essays in Memory of R.H. Lightfoot* (Oxford: Blackwell, 1967), pp. 241–62, especially pp. 251–5.

6. See in general the excellent essay by L.E. Keck, 'Ethics in the Gospel According to Matthew', *Illif Review*, 40/4 (1984), pp. 39–56.

7. Cf. M.J. Suggs, *Wisdom, Christology and Law in Matthew's Gospel* (Cambridge, Mass.: Harvard University Press, 1970).

8. Cf. E. von Dobschütz, 'Matthew as Rabbi and Catechist', in Stanton, *Interpretation*, pp. 19–29; also, D.E. Orton, *The Understanding Scribe* (Sheffield: Sheffield Academic Press, 1989).

9. So, too, A.T. Lincoln, 'Matthew—A Story for Teachers?', in D.J.A. Clines *et al.*, eds., *The Bible in Three Dimensions* (Sheffield: JSOT, 1990), pp. 103–126, esp. at p. 114.

10. Cf. also U. Luz, 'The Disciples in the Gospel According to Matthew', in Stanton, *Interpretation*, pp. 98–128. On Matt. 28:16–20 in particular, see, G. Bornkamm, 'The Risen Lord and the Earthly Jesus: Matthew 28:16–20', in J.M. Robinson, ed.,

The Future of Our Religious Past (London: SCM Press, 1971), pp. 203–229.

11. Suggestive, especially in relation to the educational process of the Cynics, is F.G. Downing, *Jesus and the Threat of Freedom* (London: SCM Press, 1987), esp. pp. 57–70. For discussion of other important parallels from the history of religions, see M. Hengel, *The Charismatic Leader and His Followers* (ET, Edinburgh: T&T Clark, 1981).

12. Cf. J.D. Kingsbury, 'The Verb *Akolouthein* ("To Follow") as an Index of Matthew's View of his Community', *Journal of Biblical Literature*, 97 (1978), pp. 56–73.

13. In general, see the excellent chapter on Matthew, in B. Gerhardsson, *The Ethos of the Bible* (ET, London: Darton, Longman & Todd, 1982), pp. 33–62.

14. Cf. S.D. Fraade, 'Ascetical Aspects of Ancient Judaism', in A. Green, ed., *Jewish Spirituality from the Bible through the Middle Ages* (London: SCM Press, 1989), pp. 253–288, noting Fraade's insightful comment on p. 276: 'Late biblical and postbiblical Judaisms, by increasing the ethical, pietistic, and legal expectations placed on the *individual*, had to find ways of dealing with the psychic and social pressures thereby created. . . . One of the ways asceticism deals with this problem is by defining discrete areas of self-control in which the individual's (and society's) will can be exercised successfully in fulfillment of transcendent purposes.'

15. On fasting in Judaism, see Davies and Allison, *Matthew*, vol. 1, pp. 356, 617f..

16. In its context in 19.1–12, it appears that the teaching is concerned primarily to deal with the case of someone who has divorced his wife on account of her unchastity: for such a man the call is to remain single and not remarry. See further, Q. Quesnell, '"Made Themselves Eunuchs for the Sake of the Kingdom of Heaven" (Matt. 19,12)', *Catholic Biblical Quarterly*, 30 (1968), pp. 335–358; also, R.H. Gundry, *Matthew: A Commentary on his Literary and Theological Art* (Grand Rapids: Eerdmans, 1982), *ad loc.*

17. Cf. most recently, D.O Via, *Self-Deception and Wholeness in Paul and Matthew* (Minneapolis: Augsburg Fortress, 1990), chs. 4–5.

18. Cf. D.J. Weaver, *Matthew's Missionary Discourse: A Literary Critical Analysis* (Sheffield: JSOT, 1990).

19. See further, Gerhardsson, *Ethos*, pp. 45–54.

20. On 18.21–35, see further, W.G. Thompson, *Matthew's Advice to a Divided Community* (Rome: Biblical Institute Press, 1970), pp. 203–237.

21. So too, Gerhardsson, *Ethos*, pp. 41–5.

22. Davies and Allison, *Matthew*, vol. 1, p. 327. The major recent study is B. Przybylski, *Righteousness in Matthew and his World of Thought* (Cambridge: Cambridge University Press, 1980).

23. Cf. Davies and Allison, *Matthew*, vol. 1, p. 499: 'So in Matthew the main problem with the Jewish leaders is not that they do not know the difference between right and wrong, it is instead that, knowing what they should do, they do something else. In view of this, 5:20 may not so much anticipate unique teaching as enjoin readers to do, to act, to be. The better righteousness is the righteousness of action—based, of course, on the words of Jesus.'

24. My translation. Compare RSV: 'Beware of practising your piety . . .'!

25. Cf. Davies and Allison, *Matthew*, vol. 1, p. 661.

26. Cf. also Via, *Self-Deception and Wholeness*, pp. 92–7.

27. Cf. M.H. Crosby, *House of Disciples: Church, Economics and Justice in Matthew* (New York: Orbis, 1988).

28. Cf. W. Trilling, *Das Wahre Israel* (Munich, 1964).

29. See further, J.A. Overman, *Matthew's Gospel and Formative Judaism* (Minneapolis: Augsburg Fortress, 1990), esp. ch. 3.

30. So, W.A. Meeks, *The Moral World of the First Christians* (London: SPCK, 1986), p. 136.

31. Meeks, *Moral World*, p. 143.

32. Meeks, *Moral World*, p. 142.

33. So too, G.N. Stanton, 'The Gospel of Matthew and Judaism', *Bulletin of the John Rylands Library*, 66 (1984), pp. 264–84.

34. See further, L.T. Johnson, 'The New Testament's Anti-Jewish Slander and the Conventions of Ancient Polemic', *Journal of Biblical Literature*, 108 (1989), pp. 419–41.

35. A good account is D.S. Russell, *The Method and Message of Jewish Apocalyptic* (London: SCM Press, 1964). Especially valuable are the essays in D. Hellholm, ed., *Apocalypticism in the Mediterranean World and the Near East* (Tübingen: Mohr/Siebeck, 1983).

36. On Matthew as responding pastorally to problems within the church, see esp. Eduard Schweizer's seminal essay, 'Observance of the Law and Charismatic Activity in Matthew', *New Testament Studies*, 16 (1970), pp. 213–230; and, more recently, P.J. Achtemeier, 'Resources for Pastoral Ministry in the Synoptic Gospels', in E.E. Shelp and R. Sutherland, eds., *A Biblical Basis for Ministry* (Philadelphia: Fortress, 1981), pp. 145–85, at 161ff..

37. J.L. Houlden, *Backward Into Light: The Passion and Resurrection of Jesus according to Matthew and Mark* (London: SCM Press, 1987), p. 60.

38. See, most recently, Overman, *Matthew's Gospel*.

39. The notable exception is B.S. Childs, *The New Testament as Canon* (London: SCM Press, 1984).

40. Note B. Gerhardsson's perceptive comment in *Ethos*, p. 33: 'A sure way to cut oneself from any possibility of understanding the structure of Jesus' and early Christianity's ethos is to begin with

the slogan "Behold I make all things new." Our sources speak an altogether different language.'

41. Argued especially by J.D. Kingsbury, in *Matthew: Structure, Christology and Kingdom* (London: SPCK, 1976).

42. But note B.S. Childs' comment, in *New Testament as Canon*, p. 78: 'However, it is equally important to observe that nowhere does Matthew transfer the name of Israel upon the church. Nor are any of the ancient titles of honour designating the people of God in the old covenant applied to the Christian community. They are not the 'elect', 'the true Israel', or the 'remnant'. Here the contrast with the Qumran community is striking. Rather, in Matthew, the imagery of the family and a household are used to describe the new community of faith (ch. 18).'

2
'For everyone will be salted with fire'

THE SPIRITUALITY OF MARK

Introduction

In studying the spirituality of the gospel of Matthew, we had an embarrassment of riches: clear and specific teaching to the community of the church on ethical matters and practices of piety as the appropriate, obedient response to the revelation of the divine presence in Jesus the Son of God. According to Matthew, the life of faith is a matter of being taught the commandments of Jesus, set out systematically in the gospel itself, and putting them into practice (cf. 28.19–20). What is left to inspiration or imagination is limited. There are answers to questions about Torah, sabbath observance, almsgiving, prayer, fasting, paying the temple tax, grounds for divorce, and so on.

By comparison, the gospel of Mark seems bare and impoverished. It is much shorter, for a start. At first glance, the teaching of Jesus seems curiously unelaborated. Typically, as at 1.21–8, we are told that Jesus' teaching is new and authoritative (1.27), but we are left in the dark as to what he says, apart from the proclamation, in a previous episode, that 'the kingdom of God is at hand' (1.15)! Here, there is no strong notion of 'discipling' as teaching and learning the commandments of Jesus, no emphasis on Jesus as the Wisdom of God (though cf. 6.2), no instruction as to what constitutes the 'greater righteousness', no clearly elaborated choice between the two ways (though cf. 8.33b), no explicit ecclesiology, no authority and disciplinary structures, and no apostolic succession to guarantee the passing on of the spiritual tradition. Perhaps most striking of all is the apparent fact that, whereas in Matthew there is such an emphasis on the fatherly presence of God and the abiding presence of Jesus, in Mark we are struck most by the hiddenness of God and, at the end, Jesus' mysterious absence.

Little wonder that Matthew should find the earlier gospel in need of drastic revision and expansion to be of more practical use as a manual for church life and missionary discipleship! Little wonder, either, that Matthew found too tenuous or undeveloped the connections in his Marcan source between the proclamation about the kingdom and its implications for prayer and daily living! In short, we are brought to the realization that Christian spirituality according to Matthew has a significantly different texture to that according to Mark.[1]

But comparisons can be irksome or unfair. It may be that the circumstances surrounding the writing of the respective gospels were so different as to necessitate quite distinct re-presentations of the story of Jesus. It may be, also, that a closer examination will show that Mark is not so reticent to depict Jesus as teacher of a way of life, as is sometimes thought.[2] Nor is it necessarily the case that the spirituality of the later, longer gospel of Matthew will be an improvement on that of its literary pre-decessor, Mark. As I suggested in the previous chapter, for example, Matthew's tendency to define what was previously ambiguous and to make transparent the opaque may be as much a concession to spiritual weakness as a mark of greater spiritual maturity.

What is required, therefore, is an attempt to describe the spirituality of the gospel of Mark, taken on its own. Sometimes it is useful to compare Mark with the other gospels, to see, for instance, developments or modifications of Mark's position, or options which he did not take up. But the prime task is to allow Mark's gospel its own integrity and to explore the vision it offers of the spiritual life under God.[3]

Marcan spirituality described

1. To begin at a point which is so basic as to be too often taken for granted, Marcan spirituality involves *a response to the revelation of God*. Of course, there is no doubt that christology bulks large in Mark, and that the proclamation of Jesus as the messiah is crucial—'The beginning of the gospel of Jesus Christ, the Son of God' is, after all, the way Mark begins (1.1). Nevertheless, behind Mark's evident christological commitment, lies a *theo*logy which is foundational for everything else.[4] A few indications of this theological underpinning are seen in the following ways.

First, the appearance of John the Baptist is presented as the fulfilment of the word of God, spoken by Isaiah (1.2–3). This means that the 'gospel' which Mark makes known begins with a statement of divine sovereignty: the fulfilment of God's will in history, with the appearance of John, as announced beforehand in scripture. Nothing happens, either for good or ill, outside God's control. That is a conviction at the very root of Marcan spirituality.

Second, at two critical points in the narrative, God's voice is heard from heaven: at the baptism (1.11), and at the transfiguration (9.7). Both occasions have to do with Jesus. The first constitutes the adoption of Jesus by God as his Son, at the very outset of his public ministry. The second comes at a turning point in the story, after Peter's christological confession at Caesarea Philippi and the initial prediction of the passion (in 8.27ff.), and reconfirms Jesus' status as the Son of God. Mark's christology is inseparable from his theology. It is God who designates Jesus as his Son. Otherwise, God is silent. He speaks and works only through intermediaries—which is the biblical pattern.[5] God himself remains transcendent and mysterious: ever-present, but only indirectly.

A third point of relevance is that Mark describes and epitomizes the message which Jesus preaches, when he comes into Galilee, as 'the gospel of *God*' (1.14); and this gospel concerns the arrival of the 'kingdom of *God*' (1.15). This means that the 'gospel', according to Mark, has a dual focus: on Jesus Christ (1.1) and on God and God's kingdom (1.14–15). Christology is not all, therefore. Rather, Jesus the messiah is the Son of God and, as God's chosen emissary, announces and inaugurates the reign of God.

A fourth point is that Jesus' exorcisms and miracles focus attention on God and Jesus' relation to God. Thus, for example, the unclean spirit identifies Jesus as the 'Holy One of God', in the very first exorcism (1.24); the healing of the paralytic provokes a controversy over whether God alone can forgive sins (2.7), and results in acclamation being given to God on account of the miracle (2.12); the demoniac Legion identifies Jesus as 'Son of the Most High God' and invokes God's name when he calls for protection (5.7); when he heals the deaf and dumb man, Jesus acknowledges the divine source of his power by 'looking up to heaven' (7.34; cf. 1.35); and when he exorcizes the demonized boy, Jesus makes the occasion a lesson in the importance of prayer to God (9.29). The exorcisms and miracles are, therefore, acts of divine power at work in and through God's emissary, Jesus. They are signals of the breaking into history of the rule of God, resulting in the binding of God's enemy, the 'strong man' Satan (3.22–7).

Finally, note how the teaching of Jesus also focuses attention on God. I have drawn attention already to Jesus' preaching the 'gospel of God' (1.14). If we ask what is the appropriate response to that gospel, the unequivocal answer comes at an important crux in the narrative, at the end of the Beelzebul controversy: '. . . whoever blasphemes against the Holy Spirit never has forgiveness . . . Whoever *does the will of God* is my brother, and sister, and mother' (3.29, 35). Right relationship with God requires doing the will of God (cf. also 7:6–9, 13), and that brings one into right relationship with Jesus too. The latter relationship presupposes the former. Immediately after, Jesus goes on to an extended parable discourse about the kingdom of God (4.1–34), where we learn, amongst other things, that God's rule is something hidden, indirect, surprising in its manifestation, and not easily perceived. That is a clue to Mark's vision of God, as well.

Jesus' teaching in Mark, then, is thoroughly theocentric. The predictions of the passion and resurrection presuppose God's sovereign and hidden purposes being worked out ('the Son of man *must* suffer many things', 8.31). When asked about the law on divorce, Jesus draws attention to the overriding intention of God: 'What therefore God has joined together, let not man put asunder' (10.9). When addressed as 'good teacher', Jesus points away from himself to 'the One God' who alone is good (10.18) and who alone, therefore, is the ground for defining good action. When teaching about entry into the kingdom of God, Jesus emphasizes that what is not possible, humanly speaking, is possible with God, 'for all things are possible with God' (10.27). When engaged in dialogue and controversy with the various parties of the Jews, it is God to whom Jesus points: the God whose kingdom surpasses that of Caesar (12.17); the God of 'the living', of Abraham, Isaac and Jacob, who has power, therefore, to raise the dead (12.24, 26–7); and the God who is One (12.29, 32) and is to be loved wholeheartedly (12.30, 33). When teaching about the end times (ch. 13), it is the divine sovereignty which is again to the fore, for it is God who makes the apocalyptic signs on the earth and in the heavens, it is 'the Lord' who shortens the days (13.20), and it is 'only the Father' who knows the timetable of future events (13.32).

From all this, we conclude that spirituality, according to Mark, has to do with *life under God*, i.e., *life as a response to the revelation of the divine*. We may characterize the God of Mark's gospel, thus. First, God is *transcendent*: he speaks from heaven (1.11) or out of the cloud on the high mountain (9.2, 7). In contrast to Matthew's anthropomorphic emphasis on God as Father, in order to convey a sense of the nearness of God to humankind, Mark speaks of God in much more reserved terms, almost entirely without attributes or ascriptions.[6] Second, God is *sovereign*: the creator of the world (10.6; 13.19), all-powerful to save (10.27), the only God (12.29), and the one who will bring history to an end (13.20). Third, God is *gracious*: he keeps his word (1.2–3); reveals knowledge of his coming (1.15) through emissaries, notably, John and Jesus (cf. 9.37); gives his Spirit (1.8, 10, etc.); gives authority to the Son of Man 'on earth' to forgive sins (2.10) and heal the sick; brings into being a new spiritual family (3.35); saves a special, elect people (13.13, 20, 27; cf. 4.10–12); gives eternal life (10.28); and overcomes suffering and death in resurrection (12.18–27; cf. 8.31; 9.31; 10.33–4).

It is this transcendent, sovereign, gracious God whom we meet in the Gospel of Mark. But there is also, fourth, *an element of unfathomable mystery*. When Jesus the Son of God dies, he dies abandoned by God. God is not present. He has forsaken him (15.34). At the point at which we might most expect the comforting presence of God, he is absent. What is more, this death is according to the will of God, as Jesus acknowledges in Gethsemane (14.36; cf. 10.45). Somehow, therefore, Jesus' experience of the absence of God is itself part of the divine purpose. It is part of what makes the death of Jesus to be 'a ransom for many'. All of this is surprising and perplexing. The surprise and perplexity is well captured in the behaviour of Peter in the Caesarea Philippi episode (8.27ff.; cf. also 14.27–31). Here, Jesus interprets messiahship as a vocation to martyrdom: 'And he said this plainly. And Peter took him, and began to rebuke him. But turning and seeing his disciples, he rebuked Peter, and said, "Get behind me, Satan! For you do not think the things of God (*ta tou theou*), but the things of men (*ta ton anthropon*)."[7] So the refusal to accept that the suffering and death of the messiah may be the will of God is satanic, in Mark's terms. It is a refusal to acknowledge God in his mysterious sovereignty.

I have tried to show that Marcan spirituality involves a response to God. It is a theistic spirituality before it is a christological one. This helps to explain a number of remarkable facets of Mark's story. First, there is the previously-mentioned saying of Jesus, in 3.35: 'Whoever does the will of God is my brother, and sister, and mother.' Not following the commandments of Jesus, as in Matthew (28.20), but obedience to the commandments of God is the primary focus (cf. 7.8–13).

Second, there is the story of the 'good scribe', in 12.28–34. When he asks Jesus, 'Which commandment is the first of all?', Jesus does not reply, 'Follow me': rather, he recites the Shema and the commandment of neighbourly love (Deut. 6.4; Lev. 19.18). The scribe commends Jesus for this response, and repeats and elaborates what Jesus has said ('. . . and to love one's neighbour as oneself, *is much more than all whole burnt offerings and sacrifices*', v. 33). In turn, Jesus says to the scribe, 'You are not far from the kingdom of God' (v. 34a). It seems legitimate to infer from this episode what is explicit in 3.35, that the primary focus for the life of faith is obedience to God.

Third, there is the story of the widow in the temple treasury (12.41–4). She is commended to the disciples by Jesus as an example of true devotion, for 'she out of her poverty has put in everything she had, her whole living (*holon ton bion*)' (v. 44b). Her devotion, be it noted, is not to Jesus, but to God, whose dwelling-place the temple is. Her behaviour is that of the pious member of God's people, and is a practical expression of the Shema.

Fourth, there is the understanding of faith in Mark's gospel. It is very striking that, of the five occurrences of *pistis* ('faith'), four are quite unqualified: 'when Jesus saw their faith' (2.5); 'Why are you afraid? Have you no faith?' (4.40); 'Daughter, your faith has made you well' (5.34); and, 'Go your way, your faith has made you well' (10.52). The fifth occurrence is qualified, and here

Jesus instructs Peter, in the context of teaching about prayer, to 'Have faith *in God*' (11.22)! When we look at the verb *pisteuein* ('to believe'), the pattern is the same. In most cases, it is used in an unqualified, absolute way. For example, 'Do not fear, only believe', says Jesus to Jairus (5.36); 'All things are possible to him who believes', says Jesus to the demoniac's father, to which he replies, 'I believe; help my unbelief!' (9.23, 24); and, 'Let the Christ . . . come down from the cross, that we may see and believe', mock the chief priests and scribes (15.32a). Only in 9.42 is there an explicit reference to believing in Jesus. Otherwise, the remaining references imply believing in God (e.g. 1.15, 'repent, and believe in the gospel', which is 'the gospel of God', according to the previous verse; cf. also, 11.23–4). In a gospel whose christological emphasis is made clear right from the opening verse, it is significant that hardly any of the *pistis/pisteuein* references focus explicitly on Jesus or on Jesus alone. Instead, faith, according to Mark, is primarily faith in God and faith in the power of God at work through Jesus.

How are we to explain this theocentric foundation in Mark? First, we can hardly doubt that it arises out of the spirituality of Jesus himself, the way Jesus lived and what he taught. So, Jesus comes proclaiming the kingdom of God and teaching about the kingdom of God in parables. Prayer to God is a constituent part of his life (1.35; 6.46; 14.22–3, 32–42; cf. 9.29; 11.17). When he goes up to Jerusalem, he purges the temple, the house of God (11.15–19). And he goes to his death as an act of obedience to the will of God (14.36).

Second, it expresses the indebtedness of early Christian spirituality to the faith of Israel and of early Judaism. The attributes of God we drew attention to earlier—transcendence, sovereignty, grace, and so on—are all thoroughly biblical and Jewish. Note, for example, Jesus' reply to the Sadducees about the resurrection: 'And as for the dead being raised, have you not read in the book of Moses, in the passage about the bush, how God said to him, "I am the God of Abraham, and the God of Isaac, and the God of Jacob"? He is not the God of the dead, but of the living; you are quite wrong' (12.26–7). There could be no clearer statement of theocentric faith, and it is indebted to the scriptures of Judaism.

Third, Mark's theocentric faith is relevant to evangelism in an

Hellenistic, polytheistic milieu (cf. 13.10: 'And the gospel must first be preached to all nations.'). Pauline monotheism provides a close analogy. In writing to the Gentile Thessalonian Christians, he reminds them of the gospel message to which they responded. A prime element in this message was the oneness of God, with the christological dimension coming only subsequently: '. . . how *you turned to God from idols, to serve a living and true God,* and to wait for his Son from heaven, whom he raised from the dead . . .' (1 Thess. 1.9–10). If this theocentric message is characteristic of the apostle to the Gentiles, it may well be that the theocentrism of the gospel expresses Mark's evangelistic and universalist concerns, as well.[8]

Finally, it is an appropriate response to the problem of persecution—namely, to provide a theodicy, an answer to experiences of suffering which grounds those experiences in beliefs about God. There can be little doubt that Mark's Gospel springs out of a context of persecution:[9] the interpretation of the parable of the sower warns of a time 'when tribulation or persecution (*diogmou*) arises on account of the word (*ton logon*)' (4.17); the reward promised to itinerant missionaries, in 10.30, is qualified by the ominous addition of the phrase, 'with persecutions'; and the little apocalypse of chapter 13 includes what has been called 'a passion prediction for Mark's community',[10] with a stark warning of hostility and persecution in both the socio-political and domestic spheres (13.9–13). In such a context, the Marcan focus on the transcendent, all-powerful God who gives life to the dead, allows his own Son to die 'as a ransom for many' (10.45), sends emissaries to all nations to preach the gospel of God, and who will intervene soon to gather the elect into the kingdom of God—this fully theocentric perspective makes good sense. It is a theodicy for suffering believers in a world at the juncture of the ages, where Satan's opposition is strong but in its terminal stage (cf. 1.24).[11]

2. If Marcan spirituality is grounded in faith in God and a response of obedience to God, it also involves *a response to Jesus the Son of God*. There is, in other words, a dual focus of Christian faith, according to Mark—something we found in Matthew also. The 'gospel' is not only 'the gospel of God' (1.14), it is also 'the gospel of Jesus Christ, the Son of God' (1.1). The

disciple is called upon by Jesus to lose his life *'for my sake* and the gospel's' (8.35b; cf. also, 10.29). On the only two occasions when God speaks, it is to (1.11) or about (9.7) Jesus his Son. The preaching of the gospel will include the story of what the anointing woman did to Jesus (14.9). Faith, according to Mark, is certainly faith in God, but it is, in particular, faith in the power of God at work in Jesus: 'What is this? A new teaching! With authority he commands even the unclean spirits, and they obey him' (1.27). Obedience to the will of God makes one a brother or sister or mother of Jesus (3.35). The miracle stories typically end with responses to Jesus which, in biblical terms, are normally reserved for responses to God: 'And they were afraid with a great fear and said to one another, "Who then is this, that the wind and the sea obey him?"' (4.41, my trans.; cf. Ps.107.23–32).[12]

The gospel as a whole leaves us with an overwhelming sense that Jesus speaks, not only to God and of God, but also that he speaks and acts *on God's behalf*. That is what is meant by the designation, 'Son of God'. That is why the designation *kurios* ('lord') is used not only of God, but of Jesus as well (e.g. 1.3; 2.28; 5.19; 12.36–7); why it is Jesus who receives the Spirit (1.10); why the disciples are summoned to follow Jesus (1.16–20; 2.14); why the demons respond to him in terror, for Jesus is God's agent for their destruction (1.24); and why God tells Peter, James and John, at the transfiguration, to *'listen to him'* (9.7b), for it is the Son who reveals to the elect the inscrutable will of God. Such examples could be multiplied. They show clearly Mark's conviction that the life of faith is theocentric and christocentric at the same time, that believing in the gospel requires believing in the God *of Jesus*.

3. The obvious question to ask in consequence is, *what does Mark's story of Jesus reveal about the nature and demands of life under God?* What is the texture of Mark's theocentric spirituality seen through the prism of Christ? In answer, we need to look first at Mark's account of what Jesus says, and second at the stories about what Jesus does and what is done to him.

There seems every reason to pay close attention to *what Jesus says*.[13] Not only does the divine voice command the privileged trio to 'listen to him' (9.7). Repeatedly, Mark draws attention to Jesus' role as one who gives 'teaching' (*didache*), the introduction to the parable discourse of chapter 4 being a good example: 'And he began *to teach* beside the sea. . . . And he *taught* them many things in parables, and *in his teaching* he said to them . . .' (4.1–2).[14] Repeatedly, Jesus is addressed in the vocative as 'Teacher', sometimes even when he is not engaged in teaching.[15] Also, Mark often draws attention to the authority (*exousia*) of Jesus as a teacher and to the power of his words: 'And they were astonished at his teaching, for he taught them as one who had authority, and not as the scribes' (1.22; cf. 1.27; 2.10; 11.27–33). We do well to note, yet further, that Jesus is commonly depicted engaging in long teaching sessions (cf. 4.1–34; 7.1–23; 9.30–50; 10.17–31; 11.27–12.44; 13.1–37), a fact sometimes overlooked due to the impact of the great discourses of the gospels of Matthew or John. Most striking is the deeply ironic encomium placed on the lips of the hostile Pharisees and Herodians, at the beginning of a cycle of controversy stories: 'Teacher, we know that you are true, and care for no man; for you do not regard the position of men, *but truly teach the way of God*' (12.14a). Jesus' role and authority as teacher of the will of God could receive no stronger accolade, even if the speakers themselves do not believe it, such is their spiritual blindness.

If, therefore, Mark highlights Jesus as teacher with authority of the way of God, it is likely that he wants to give particular prominence to what Jesus says. This may be because Mark intends that the teaching of Jesus should interpret the deeds of Jesus: above all, that the teaching of Jesus about the suffering Son of Man should qualify the incipient triumphalism of the miracle stories.[16] But this could only be a partial explanation. More obvious is the suggestion that Mark believes that Jesus the divine Son authoritatively reveals the will of God, reveals what the dawning of the kingdom of God means and how to live in its light. We need, therefore, to try to spell out some of the main aspects of this teaching.

First, we turn to the carefully crafted, central section of the gospel, 8.27–10.45.[17] Here, Jesus is 'on the way (*en te hodo*)' (8.27; 9.33f.; 10.32) to Jerusalem and the passion. The teaching he imparts on the journey is at the very heart of Mark's understanding of christology and its implications for disciples in the life of faith. Three times Jesus teaches that the Son of Man must suffer and rise from the dead (8.31; 9.31; 10.33–4), and each time he instructs the disciples on the implications of the passion for discipleship. So christology and discipleship are linked inextricably. This of itself is an important point. It is as if Mark is saying that belief matters—specifically, that what you believe about Christ bears directly upon how you live. For Mark, Jesus the Christ, the Son of God is, above all, *the suffering Son of Man*. Thus, the whole central section ends with the saying: 'For the Son of man also came not to be served but to serve, and to give his life as a ransom for many' (10.45). But this is a hard lesson to learn, for it involves the deeply unworldly notion that the power of God and of the Son of God is revealed in the death of the Son of Man, and that true discipleship lies in the practice, not of saving your life, but of losing it (cf. 8.34–5; 9.33–7; 10.35–45). This is why the teaching has to be imparted three times, and its implications spelt out and elaborated.

For Mark, then, being a disciple is about following Jesus, the suffering Son of Man, in the way of the cross. *Christian spirituality is cruciform*: 'And he called to him the multitude with his disciples, and said to them, "If any man would come after me, let him deny himself and take up his cross and follow me. For whoever would save his life will lose it; and whoever loses his life for my sake and the gospel's will save it"' (8.34–5). This is *the* most important aspect of Marcan spirituality. That is why this teaching comes at the opening of the central section, after the first passion prediction. Note also that it functions as an elaboration of the rebuke to the leading disciple, Peter; and indicates what thinking 'the things of God (*ta tou theou*)' ought to involve (cf. v. 33). Note further, that Jesus addresses the teaching to 'the multitude with his disciples' (v. 34a), and that the teaching has a consistently generalizing form: 'If any one . . . For whoever . . . and whoever . . .' (vv. 34–5; cf. also v. 38). So this teaching is understood by Mark to be applicable and relevant beyond the particular, historical circumstances of the passion of Jesus.[18] It expresses the essence of life under God and in response to Christ for Mark's readers, as well. Such teaching would be especially important in a context of persecution as a result of witness to Christ; and this is implicit in the idea of losing your life 'for my sake and the gospel's' (v. 35), in the warning against being ashamed 'of me and of my words' when (presumably) called to give account (cf. 13.9–11), and in the reference to 'tasting death', in 9.1. It may be that Mark places such weight on this teaching because the temptation is strong among his readers to avoid suffering and persecution at any cost and, like Peter (14.66–72), to deny allegiance to Christ.

We must deal more briefly with other aspects of the Marcan Jesus' teaching about discipleship in this central section. For following Jesus in the way of the cross has certain corollaries. First, such following means that *present experiences of heavenly glory are limited and transitory* (9.2–8), and that anticipations of eschatological restoration are only anticipations (9.11–13). The privileged trio have to come down from the 'high mountain' where they have seen the transfiguration, and they are not to speak about it 'until the Son of man should have risen from the dead' (9.9). Similarly, the eschatological Elijah has come, in the person of John the Baptist, but he was brutally killed (cf. 6.14–29), and the Son of Man has yet to be 'treated with contempt' (9.12). Triumph and exaltation, therefore, lie well and truly in the future, on the other side of suffering for the sake of Christ and the gospel.[19]

Second, life in the interim demands *unwavering faith in the all-powerful God, expressed in prayer*. Only prayer will make possible the conquest of the forces of spiritual darkness in the world. That is the note on which the remarkable and extended exorcism story of 9.14–29 ends. Not acclamation of Jesus' power as Son of God, which is what we might have expected after such a dramatic exorcism (note vv. 18, 20, 25–7), but teaching in private (which has all the hallmarks of Marcan redaction)[20] that, 'This kind cannot be driven out by anything but prayer' (9.28–29). For Mark, the spiritual life will involve necessarily a fierce conflict with satanic forces which can be overcome only by prayer. And prayer, as an expression of faith in God, is a theme to which the Marcan Jesus returns, in 11.20–25: 'Therefore I tell you, whatever you ask in prayer, believe that you have received it, and it will be yours' (v. 24). Prayer, also, is the practice of Jesus himself, which allows him to overcome the weakness of the flesh, in the garden of Gethsemane (14.32–42, noting v. 38). So it is clearly a significant aspect of Marcan spirituality, a practical outworking of theocentric and christocentric faith.

A third corollary of following the suffering Son of Man has to do with *relations among the followers*. This matter is covered in a series of loosely connected units of tradition, in 9.33–50.[21] That these traditional units are related specifically to discipleship of the Son of Man is evident from the fact that they follow immediately upon the second prediction of the passion of the Son of Man (9.30–2), and they are introduced by editorial material containing the key discipleship catchphrase, 'on the way' (vv. 33b, 34b). So, it is with considerable irony that it is while they are 'on the way' to Jerusalem with the one who 'came not to be served but to serve (*diakonesai*)' (10.45), that they are found to be discussing among themselves who is the greatest! Jesus' reply, seated as a teacher (v. 35a), is that the one who wants to be first must be 'last of all and servant (*diakonos*) of all', and that such service is to be demonstrated in various ways: in the practice of welcoming outsiders, such as itinerant missionaries[22] into the fellowship (vv. 36–7); in not hindering the work of an anonymous Christian exorcist (vv. 38–40) or refusing an outsider's hospitality (v. 41); and in taking great care not to cause a fellow believer to apostasize (vv. 42–50). The common thread here is that of humility and a willingness to serve the other; or, to put it slightly differently, 'the truly great will not define the borders of the Christian fellowship so that it includes only themselves.'[23]

Yet a fourth corollary of following the suffering Son of Man has to do with *household relations*. These are touched upon in another sequence of traditional units, in 10.1–31, which deal successively with marriage and divorce (vv. 2–12), children (vv. 13–16), and property (vv. 17–31). What is important to note, however, is that the teaching of the Marcan Jesus on matters such as these is not casuistic. That is a development which begins to appear in Matthew, where, for example, in that gospel's version, the teaching on divorce becomes a matter of defining what are legitimate grounds for divorce. The Pharisees ask, 'Is it lawful to divorce one's wife *for any cause*?'; and Jesus replies, 'I say to you, whoever divorces his wife, *except for unchastity*, and marries another, commits adultery' (Matt. 19.3, 9; cf. 5.32). In Mark, the central issue is, what is the fundamental will of God: for God is sovereign and his kingdom is imminent. So, divorce is ruled out, because the will of God 'from the beginning of creation' is for lifelong marriage. Children are to be welcomed into the fellowship of God's people, because the kingdom of God belongs to such as they. And attachment to possessions is to be made subordinate to attachment to Jesus, because it is Jesus who leads the way into the kingdom of God. Not a casuistic spirituality, therefore, but a theological and eschatological spirituality is what we find in Mark: 'an ethical issue is raised only to be settled at the level of theology rather than of ethics. For Mark, the answer to the question, "What is my duty with regard to X?" is, "God is sovereign—live under his rule."[24]

Implicit in the teaching of Jesus in this central section of Mark is that the kingdom of God inaugurated by and embodied in the suffering Son of Man requires *a basic change in outlook and expectations*. What is quite understandable from a human point of view is shown up to be totally wide of the mark, even satanic (cf. 8.33)! Instead, the Son of Man '*must* suffer'; the follower of Jesus must 'take up his cross'; the greatest must become servant (9.35) and even slave (10.44) of all; to enter the kingdom, you have to receive it 'like a child' (10.15); and the last will be first and the first last (two instances: 9.35b and 10.31). This change in outlook is hard won. Not even Jesus' most intimate disciples attain it. Thus, in the final episode of the central section (10.35–45), immediately following the third and most explicit passion prediction, 'on the way, going up to Jerusalem' (10.32–4), we find James·and John still, mentally and spiritually, on the Mount of Transfiguration, still fixated on 'glory': 'Grant us to sit, one at your right hand and one at your left, in your glory' (v. 37). What they are offered instead are two metaphors of sacrifice—the cup and baptism—as well as the word about the Son of Man who gives his life 'as a ransom for many' (v. 45).

Moving beyond the teaching of Jesus in the central section of Mark, we find further elaboration elsewhere of what it means to believe in the gospel and follow the suffering Son of Man. One important issue has to do with *the role of the law*. In Matthew, the teaching of Jesus is interpreted as upholding, fulfilling and deepening the covenantal demands of the law (e.g. Matt. 5.17–20). There is a real sense in which Matthean spirituality is nomistic and even casuistic. In Mark, the situation is considerably different, however. The overwhelming sense here is of the freedom and re-formation of life as God's people which the breaking in of the kingdom brings.[25] Thus, the teaching of Jesus is 'a new teaching (*didache kaine*) with authority' (1.27; omitted by Matthew).

When Jesus instructs the healed leper to 'offer for your cleansing what Moses commanded' (1.44), it is noteworthy that the leper does not do so, but goes away and 'preaches freely and spreads the word' instead (1.45a), an aspect of the story which Matthew omits, presumably because it appears antinomian (Matt. 8.4)! When Jesus is accused of infringing purity rules by eating with 'tax collectors and sinners', his reply is blunt and to the point: '. . . I came not to call the righteous, but sinners' (2.17). Matthew evidently feels the need to legitimate such a stance from Scripture, in order (once more) to soften what might be interpreted as an antinomian stance, so he adds the appeal to Hos. 6.6 ('I desire mercy, and not sacrifice'). Where the Marcan Jesus concludes the metaphor of the wineskins with, 'new wine is for fresh skins' (2.22), the Jesus of Matthew ends on the more conservative note, 'so both are preserved' (9.17). In Mark's version of the controversy over plucking grain on the sabbath, Jesus concludes by saying that, 'The sabbath was made for man, not man for the sabbath . . .' (2.27). This was too much for Matthew. Not only does he bolster Jesus' defence of the disciples' action by an additional appeal to the law (Matt. 12.5–7): he also omits the Marcan statement, with its appearance of a drastic relativization of sabbath law, altogether (cf. also Mark 13.18 par. Matt. 24.20). Yet again, in the dispute with the Pharisees over the things that defile, Mark draws the conclusion from the sayings of Jesus that, 'Thus he declared all foods clean' (7.19b). Matthew must have found such a wholesale demolition of the Levitical purity rules (cf. Lev. 11; Deut. 14) a *tour de force*, to say the least. So he omits the Marcan commentary, and ends the pericope in a way which indicates that, in his view, only the traditional teaching about eating with hands unwashed has been set aside by Jesus (Matt. 15.20). To sum up, Allen Verhey puts the matter well: 'Whatever else discipleship requires, it evidently provided a significant freedom from scrupulous observance of the regulations of the Jewish authorities, according to Mark. . . . All such regulations belong to the past, not to the eschatological community oriented to watchful discipleship. . . . The norm is no longer the precepts of Moses but the Lord and his words (8.38).'[26]

If Marcan spirituality is not casuistic, it is not sacerdotal, either. If the lawyers are marginalized, so are the temple and the cult.[27] Jesus comes to the temple, at the culmination of his ministry, not to worship there, but to bring proceedings to a standstill: 'and he would not allow any vessel (*skeuos*) to be carried through the temple' (11.16, my trans.).[28] Significantly, Mark then says that Jesus 'taught (*edidasken*), and said to them, "Is it not written, 'My house shall be called a house of prayer for all the nations'? . . ."' (11.17); and the episode ends with Mark noting the mortal enmity of the chief priests and scribes and, on the other hand, the astonishment of the multitude 'at his teaching (*epi te didache autou*)' (11.18).[29] Clearly, Jesus' teaching, both about the temple and in the temple (cf. 11.27ff.; 12.35ff., 41; 13.1ff.; 14.49), is especially important to Mark. And there can be no doubt that the judgment of Jesus about the temple is negative.[30] Like the fig tree (11.12–14, 20–5), the temple and the cult are barren.[31] Because the temple has not fulfilled its purpose as 'a house of prayer for all the nations', its days are numbered. This is made explicit, both at the beginning of the apocalyptic discourse, at 13.1–2; and also at the trial (14.58) and crucifixion (15.29; cf. also v. 38).[32] The sovereignty of God and the coming of his kingdom according to Mark, transcend not only Moses, but the temple cult as well. God is now to be found in and through the crucified Son (15.39).

But there is an important element in the teaching of the Marcan Jesus which has yet to be considered and which helps to give us some idea of what takes the place of casuistry and cult in the spirituality of Mark. What I have in mind here is the *eschatological dimension* of Marcan spirituality. Put briefly, casuistry is unnecessary and the cult is superseded because the kingdom of God is 'at hand' (1.15).[33] What is important now is the preaching of the gospel to all nations (13.10; cf. 14.9) and being willing to leave everything for the sake of Jesus and the gospel (cf. 10.28–30) in the short time that remains before the kingdom of God comes 'with power' (9.1).

The eschatological teaching of Jesus in chapter 13 is central here, because it is a private revelation (v. 3) about future events, clearly addressed to the situation of Jesus' followers in the period after the passion and resurrection of the Son of Man and intended to prepare them for it.[34] From this teaching, we can draw important inferences about Marcan spirituality. First, it is a spirituality oriented on *hope for the imminent future*: 'And then they will see the Son of man coming in clouds with great power and glory. . . . So also, when you see these things taking place, you know that he is near, at the very gates. Truly, I say to you, this generation will not pass away before all these things take place' (13.26, 29–30; cf. 9.1). To use Frank Kermode's phrase, the gospel of Mark has a strong 'sense of an ending',[35] and this has a powerful relativizing effect upon all other attachments and commitments, as well as upon casuistry and cult.

Second, it is a spirituality demanding a *heightened degree of attentiveness*: what Verhey calls, 'watchful discipleship.'[36] This is evident from the unique conglomeration of verbs for 'seeing' or 'watching' in this discourse: *blepein* occurs five times (vv. 2, 5, 9, 23, 33), *gregorein* three times (vv. 34, 35, 37), *horan* once (v. 26), *agrupnein* also once (v. 33), and the imperative *ide* ('behold!') occurs three times (v. 1, and twice in v. 21). It is evident also in the fact that the discourse comes to a climax around the theme of the imperative of watchfulness, with a definite generalizing of the message at the end: 'Take heed, watch; for you do not know when the time will come. . . . Watch, therefore . . . lest he come suddenly and find you asleep. And what I say to you *I say to all*: Watch' (vv. 33–37). So Mark's Gospel is a summons to vigilance, to stay awake and not to fall asleep in view of the imminent end. This message is reinforced immediately in the narrative which follows, a narrative which functions as an anticipation of the events of the end.[37] The anonymous woman in the house of Simon shows that she is 'awake', by seizing the moment and anointing Jesus for his burial (14.3–9). In Gethsemane, by contrast, Jesus asks Peter, James and John to 'watch (*gregoreite*)' (14.34), but three times he comes and finds them asleep (14.37, 40, 41). And later that same night, in spite of the threefold instruction to 'watch' (in 13.33–7) and his failure to 'watch' in Gethsemane, Peter denies his master three times (14.66–72).

Why does Mark place such heavy emphasis on the need for vigilance? Mainly, because the short time before the end and the parousia of the Son of Man is a time of heightened spiritual and physical danger. There is the danger of being 'led astray' by false messiahs and false prophets (13.5–6, 21–2), the threat of persecution for the sake of allegiance to the name of Jesus (13.9–13), and the perils associated with the cosmic 'birthpangs' which bring this age to an end and usher in the age to come (13.7–8, 14–19). There is, too, the danger of not being prepared to stand up and be counted when the moment of testing comes (14.27ff., 66–72). As Jesus says to the disciples: 'Watch and pray that you may not enter into temptation; the spirit indeed is willing, but the flesh is weak' (14.38). For Mark, the world is a hostile place inhabited by demonic powers (cf. 1.13, 24; 3.22–7; 5.1–20; etc.) and wicked rulers (cf. 6.14–29; 13.9) who are in their death-throes with the advent of God's rule and God's messiah. The time before their final overthrow is a time of intense struggle of cosmic proportions. In order not to succumb in the struggle, therefore, the disciple of Jesus is warned in advance to 'watch' and 'stay awake'.

But this attentiveness has another side to it, as well. Not just spiritual vigilance is required, but *spiritual insight* as well.[38] The two are linked closely. At the linguistic level, *blepein* is used, in Mark, in both senses. The best examples of *blepein* as spiritual insight come, significantly, in the earlier discourse in chapter 4 which parallels in many ways that in chapter 13. Says Jesus, once again in private revelation to a select group (4.10ff.): 'To you has been given the secret of the kingdom of God, but for those outside everything is in parables; so that "*seeing they may see* but not perceive, and hearing they may hear and not understand; lest they should turn again and be forgiven"' (lit. trans.). Also, in 4.24, again in the context of the parables and their interpretation, Jesus begins the little parable of the measure by saying, *blepete ti akouete*: 'See [in the sense of "understand"] what you hear'. Yet further, in 8.17–18, Jesus rebukes the disciples' lack of understanding about the loaves, with the words: 'Do you not yet perceive or understand? Are your hearts hardened? "Having eyes *do you not see*, and having ears do you not hear?" And do you not remember?' It is as if Mark wants his readers to recognize that the intense vigilance required in the times of testing before the kingdom comes will be possible only for those whose spiritual insight is finely tuned, or, to put it another way, only for those who understand the parable of the sower (4.3–20, noting esp. v. 13). For only those people will recognize 'the hour' when it comes; only they will be able to discern true prophecy from false and not be 'led astray'; only they will be able to receive the perplexing and testing will of God and do it.

Having given some attention to what Jesus *says*, according to Mark, we turn now to stories about *what Jesus does and what is done to Jesus*. This will serve as a basis for further inferences about Mark's understanding of life under God in response to the revelation of Christ.

The baptism of Jesus by John in the Jordan is the first story about Jesus in Mark (1.9–11), so it must be significant.[39] In fact, it is a cameo of the gospel story as a whole, for it connects with the story of the passion, at the end. Thus, the baptism anticipates his baptism in death, of which he speaks, in 10.38ff.: 'Are you able . . . to be baptized with the baptism with which I am baptized?' (cf. Rom. 6.3ff.). The rending of the heavens anticipates the rending of the temple curtain when Jesus dies: only in 1.10 and 15.38 does the word *schizein* ('to tear apart') occur in Mark. And the identification of Jesus as God's Son (1.11) anticipates the confession of the centurion at the cross that, 'This man was the Son of God' (15.39). From the very outset of his ministry, therefore, *Jesus' life bears the marks of the passion*. Jesus' exaltation as the divine Son is by way of the cross, from beginning to end. So what he teaches about discipleship, he embodies in his own life.

The temptation in the wilderness is equally significant as an epitome of the gospel as a whole (1.12–13). Note that Jesus is 'driven' (*ekballein*) into the wilderness by the Spirit, the same Spirit which descended upon him at his baptism (1.10). Jesus' wilderness testing is not by chance, therefore: rather, it is the divine will. Just as God tested his 'son' Israel in the wilderness for forty years (cf. Deut. 8), so now he tests his Son, Jesus. *The vocation and election are followed by the testing*. That is the biblical pattern.[40] It is the pattern for Jesus. It will be the pattern for those who follow Jesus, as well. This testing involves Jesus' first confrontation with Satan. That, rather than the nature of the temptations (as in Matthew and Luke), is what Mark emphasizes. He does so because he wants to make clear from the start that *life under God involves struggle with demonic powers*; and, for Jesus, this struggle continues in the exorcism stories and in the Passion (cf. 8.33). But Jesus does not struggle with the

57

demonic unaided, for 'angels ministered to him'. Along with the blunt sobriety of Mark's opening, there is a note of hope and encouragement, as well.

Having faithfully endured the testing by Satan, Jesus is prepared for his mission and comes into Galilee preaching the gospel (1.15–16). He can announce with assurance that the kingdom of God is near, because he himself has experienced the conflict with, and conquest over, Satan, in the wilderness. The events then follow in quick and abrupt succession, frequently punctuated by the adverb, 'immediately' (*euthus*), which occurs 42 times in Mark as a whole, of which eleven occurrences come in chapter 1, and all but ten come in the first half of the Gospel (i.e. 1.1–8:26). The overwhelming sense is one of action and urgency with strong eschatological overtones. The end is near; there is no time to lose. The gospel must be preached 'first' (cf. 13.10).

It is no coincidence that Jesus' first preaching is followed by the call of disciples who leave everything 'immediately' and 'follow'/'go after' him (1.16–20). The episode epitomizes what life under God now means with the coming of Christ and the announcement of the kingdom. It means *following Jesus and becoming agents of the kingdom of God even at the cost of occupation and family ties* (cf. 10.28–30; 13.9–12).[41] The theme of discipleship as 'following' Jesus in response to his authoritative word of call, introduced in 1.16–20, is all-pervasive in Mark.[42] Along with the cross, this is the central metaphor of the spiritual life in this Gospel. So, Simon and Andrew and James and John, a core group within the Twelve, are called to 'follow' (*akolouthein*); Levi, not one of the Twelve, is called likewise (2.14); and, in 8.34, after the first passion prediction, Jesus issues the invitation to all, in a way which is intended clearly to be an address to the readers of Mark's gospel as well. Here, *akolouthein* occurs, emphatically, twice: 'If any one wants *to follow* after me, let him deny himself and take up his cross, and *follow* me' (my trans.). What this 'following' is about deserves a little further attention.

First, we notice that *it is a path or journey metaphor*. This makes it especially important for our inquiry into Marcan spirituality, for path and journey metaphors are very common ways of describing the life of faith, from scriptural times to Bunyan's *Pilgrim's Progress* and beyond. In Mark itself,

58

'following' is associated specifically with Jesus as the one who is 'on the way (*en te hodo*)' and who 'goes before' (*proagein*).[43] In particular, the important central section of Mark is carefully constructed as a journey, beginning at Caesarea Philippi and ending with the ascent to Jerusalem. During the course of this journey, Jesus is described repeatedly as being 'on the way' or 'going ahead', with the disciples (and not just the Twelve) 'following' him. And it is on the journey that Jesus teaches his followers about the suffering of the Son of Man and the corollaries of this christology for discipleship. Notably, each of the three passion predictions coincides with an occurrence of the phrase, 'on the way' (cf. 8.27; 9.33–4; 10.32). So the journey is not just a progression of the topographic kind. It is even more, and at the same time, a journey of revelation and spiritual encounter. Only thus can we explain the language of epiphany, the 'fear' and 'amazement',[44] which characterizes the response of the disciples as they follow: 'And they were *on the way* (*en te hodo*) going up to Jerusalem, and Jesus was *going before* (*proagon*) them; and *they were amazed* (*ethambounto*), and *those who followed* (*hoi akolothountes*) *were afraid* (*ephobounto*)' (10.32). The way of the Son of Man, going before his followers to Jerusalem to die as 'a ransom for many' in obedience to the divine will, is a prospect of *aweful* dimensions, in both senses of that word. It can be received only as a revelation, and it can be 'followed' only with divine aid (cf. 10.23–7). Following Jesus, therefore, means journeying on the way with Jesus, a way which is revelatory, which leads to cross-bearing, and through cross-bearing to resurrection vindication (cf. 16.7: 'He is *going before* (*proagei*) you to Galilee; there you will see him . . .').

Second, this following on the way is *open to people of all kinds*. It is as if the journeying with the suffering Son of Man makes possible the crossing of normally fixed boundaries and barriers which are not so much geographical, as social and religious and spiritual.[45] This helps to explain Mark's fondness for highlighting the activity of Jesus among the crowds and the responsiveness (but notoriously fickle responsiveness) of the crowds to Jesus. Typical is the Marcan summary statement, in 3.7ff.: 'And a great multitude from Galilee followed; also from Judea and Jerusalem and Idumea and from beyond the Jordan and from about Tyre and Sidon a great multitude, hearing all that he did, came to him.'[46] Jesus' concern is universal (cf. 13.10), and access to him is universal also. Hence, those who 'follow' include Galilean fishermen, tax collectors and sinners (2.13–17), a healed demoniac (5.1–20, noting vv. 18–20), a Gentile centurion (15.39), and many Galilean women (15.40–41). Very striking is the fact that these are what we might call the 'little people' of the day,[47] those excluded from power and recognition by virtue of their geographic origins, type of work, state of health, gender, or nationality.

The story of blind Bartimaeus epitomizes this point (10.46–52). If it was once a simple miracle story, it becomes in Mark's hands a story about discipleship available to all. It comes at the end of the major central section on christology and discipleship, and functions as a summation of it. In particular, it serves as an illustration of the climactic saying in 10.45: for this blind man represents 'the many' for whom the Son of Man gives his life. From being a blind beggar outside the city, sitting 'beside the way (*para ten hodon*)', he becomes, by his active and persistent faith in Jesus the Son of David, one who receives his sight and, leaving behind his beggar's mantle, *follows (akolouthein)* Jesus 'on the way (*en te hodo*)', the way to Jerusalem and the cross (cf. 11.1).

Of course, if following Jesus on the way is open to all and has a tendency to transcend taken-for-granted boundaries and divisions, it should be said, as a third point, that *such following is counter-cultural and generates conflict with supporters of the status quo*. This is why Mark's story of Jesus is conflict-ridden.[48] John the Baptist announces 'the way' (1.2–3) and ends up in conflict with Herod and mercilessly executed (6.14–29). His passion, narrated at remarkable length in between the departure of the apostles on mission and their return (6.7–13, 30ff.), serves as a warning of what all of God's emissaries should expect from the powers-that-be (cf. 13.10), and anticipates the passion of Jesus at the hands of the Jewish and Roman authorities.

Jesus too is cast as a controversialist. Witness, for instance, the corresponding cycles of controversy stories, at the beginning and end of the gospel (2.1–3.6; 11.27–12.37), which bring upon Jesus the mortal enmity of the leading groups (cf. 3.6; 14.1–2; also, 12.12, 13). Witness also the tension and misunderstanding between Jesus and his relatives (3.20–1, 31–5), and the episode of Jesus' rejection in his home town (6.1–6). Then too, there are the expressions of Jesus' prophetic anger: anger with Satan at his disfigurement of the man with leprosy (1.41);[49] anger at the hardness of heart of the Pharisees who would not have Jesus heal the man with the withered hand on the sabbath (3.1–6, at v. 5; omitted by Matthew and Luke); and anger at the abuse of the temple cult by the exclusion of the Gentiles (11.11, 15–19), mentioned earlier. Finally, witness the extensive narrative of the trials of Jesus and the crucifixion which bears eloquent witness to the perception of Jesus as a subversive and a trouble-maker by those in authority (e.g. 14.43–50, noting v. 48; 14.53–65, noting v. 58).

The story of the anointing woman, at the beginning of the Passion (14.3–9), exemplifies the counter-cultural and conflictual nature of this following on the way.[50] Significantly, the anointing is the spontaneous and generous action of an anonymous woman: it contrasts with the murderous and deceitful actions of leading men, references to whom frame the story (14.1–2, 10–11). Jesus is anointed on his head (v. 3): so the event has messianic overtones, as of the anointing of a king (cf. 1 Sam. 10.1; 2 Kings 9.3, 6). But the anointing of this king takes place, not in the temple in Jerusalem, but in a leper's house in Bethany (v. 3); and it is performed, not by the high priest, but by the woman. Her silent action generates conflict: 'they reproached (*enebrimonto*) her' for wasting money (v. 5). But the defence of her action by Jesus shows that this reproach is crass and short-sighted. For what the woman has done is a statement of the way of the cross: 'she has anointed my body beforehand for burying' (v. 8). It expresses the sacrificial and counter-cultural following of the suffering Son of Man which is of the essence of the gospel. That is why Jesus commends her in a way unprecedented of anyone else in this gospel: '. . . wherever the gospel is preached in the whole world, what she has done will be told in memory of her' (v. 9).

I have discussed the meaning of following Jesus on the way at length, because it is at the heart of Marcan spirituality. To put it in other words, the life of faith requires the *imitatio Christi* (cf. 8.34). This *imitatio Christi* spirituality has an *active dimension* to it, just as the life of the Marcan Jesus has an active dimension. Jesus is an *exorcist* (cf. 1.32ff.; 3.11f.).[51] Think of the man in the synagogue (1.21–8), the Gerasene demoniac (5.1–20), the little daughter of the Syrophoenician woman (7.24–30), and the demonized boy whom the disciples cannot heal (9.14–29). Jesus is a *healer* also. Think of Simon's mother-in-law (1.29–31), the leper (1.40–5), the paralytic (2.1–12), the man with the withered hand (3.1–6), the Gerasene demoniac (5.1–20), the daughter of Jairus and the woman with the haemorrhage (5.21–43), the deaf mute in the Decapolis (7.31–7), and the blind men, one at Bethsaida (8.22–6), the other outside Jericho (10.46–52). In addition, Jesus is an *itinerant preacher and teacher*, as we saw earlier; and *a prophet* as well (e.g. ch. 13). He rises early and seeks out a lonely place to pray (1.35). He eats and drinks with 'sinners' (2.15–17), provides food for the multitudes (6.30–44; 8.1–10), and shares the Passover with his disciples (14.12–25). In all these ways and more, Jesus' life as God's obedient Son is characterized by action, by *doing things with others and for others*. As Jesus himself says, 'The Son of man came not to be served but to serve . . .' (10.45). Mark's intention in so portraying Jesus is to present him as a model for followers. They too are to be active doers of the will of God (cf. 3.35), preaching and teaching, healing and exorcizing (cf. 3.13ff; 6.7–13, 30; 13.10), and taking up their crosses (8.34).

But the *imitatio Christi* has a *passive dimension* to it, as well, for that is another aspect of the life of the Marcan Jesus. As William Vanstone has shown,[52] the use of the verb *paradidomi* ('hand over', 'deliver up') is especially indicative of this passive dimension of the ministry of Jesus and of Christian discipleship. Thus, it is used of John (1.14), of Jesus (9.31; 10.33; etc.), and of followers of Jesus (13.9, 11, 12). In every occurrence, it refers, not to something which John or Jesus or disciples do, but to something which is done to them. The overwhelming concentration of occurrences comes in the passion narrative. Here, therefore, we note a striking change. From being so active, the Jesus of Mark becomes passive, acted upon.[53] The verb is central to the second and third of the three passion predictions (9.31; 10.33); it comes three times in the passion prediction for the community (13.9, 11, 12); and then ten times in the passion narrative proper (14.10, 11, 18, 21, 41, 42, 44; 15.1, 10, 15). So we may fairly say that the Passion involves Jesus in being at the receiving end of the actions of others, being 'handed over', powerless, even forsaken (15.34). But paradoxically, this passivity, this being acted upon, is the will of God (8.31) and is salvific. It is in the losing of his life at the hands of others that the Son of Man becomes 'a ransom for many' (10.45). So too for the disciple. It is in the losing of his or her life for the sake of Jesus and the gospel, that he or she saves it (8.35b). Here, then, is *a spirituality for the persecuted, the powerless, the 'done to'*. Mark's message for his persecuted community corresponds closely with the message given by the risen Lord to the suffering and persecuted apostle, Paul: 'My grace is sufficient for you, for my power is made perfect in weakness' (2 Cor. 12.9).

Conclusion

I have tried to describe the main elements of Marcan spirituality in so far as they may be inferred from the way in which Mark presents and interprets the story of Jesus. It is important now, however briefly, to suggest at least one area where further thought might be given and to ask if there are points at which Mark's understanding of the life of faith leaves something to be desired or raises questions which Mark himself does not answer.

The main issue I wish to raise has to do with the observation that Marcan spirituality is *a dark, strenuous spirituality*. It is a gospel of the Passion from beginning to end: 'For everyone will be salted with fire' (9.49; Mark only). John the Baptist, Jesus, and the followers of Jesus all go (or are meant to go) the way of suffering. The final words of Jesus the teacher of the kingdom of God are the cry of abandonment by God (15.34). To put it another way, there is not much joy: in contrast to Matthew, where beatitude and joy abound, and to Luke-Acts, where the motif of joy and rejoicing is all pervasive.[54] The word for 'joy', *chara*, occurs just once, in the interpretation of the parable of the sower (at 4.16): but it is used of those whose reception of the word is superficial, so that they fall away quickly in the face of persecution because 'they have no root in themselves' (4.17). Similarly, *chairo* ('rejoice', 'be glad') occurs only in 14.11, and there it is used of the exultation of the chief priests at the willingness of Judas to betray Jesus!

If there is not much joy, there is not much humour, either. What humour there is, is of the distinctly serious kind—irony in particular, which allows the insider to nod knowingly, but leaves the outsider in the dark. So, for example, the mock coronation of Jesus by the battalion of soldiers in the praetorium prior to the crucifixion (15.16–20), or the mocking words of the scribes at the foot of the cross, 'He saved others; he cannot save himself. Let the Christ, the King of Israel, come down now from the cross, that we may see and believe' (15.31–2). Even here, we notice that the focus of the irony, with its distinctly bitter taste, is the Passion.

The portrayal of the twelve in Mark reinforces this sense. Following Jesus on the way is so strenuous, so opaque, that not even Jesus' chosen intimates make the grade. The recurring pattern is one of revelation to the disciples followed by misunderstanding, ignorance, forgetfulness, and even cowardice. After the two great feeding miracles, they do not understand (8.17–21); after each passion prediction, they show themselves blind and hard-hearted (e.g. 8.32–3); after Jesus' prophetic protest in the temple, they can only marvel at the magnificence of the temple buildings (13.1); Peter denies him; Judas betrays him; and they all run away when he is arrested (14.50), never again to reappear in person in the narrative. The portrayal leaves us with a sense of almost unrelieved gloom.[55] There is no room for boasting here. The apostle Paul would have understood well (cf. 2 Cor. 10–13).

Yet another aspect of this is the way Mark orders the miracle stories.[56] These great demonstrations of divine power, like the stilling of the storm (4.35–41) or the miraculous feedings (6.30–44; 8.1–10), nearly all occur in the first half of Mark. If they occur in the central section, they have turned into stories about discipleship (e.g. 10.46–52). After that, with Jesus' arrival at Jerusalem, where he is to be crucified, there is only one further miracle, and that is a judgment one, the cursing of the fig tree (11.12–14, 20ff.). The result of this is that the triumphal effect of the miracle stories is qualified massively by the narrative of the Passion, a muzzling process which begins even earlier with Jesus' constant injunctions to 'say nothing to anyone' (e.g. 1.25, 34, 44; 3.12; 5.43; etc.). Even the transfiguration takes place only in the presence of Peter, James and John, and they are told 'to tell no one what they had seen, *until the Son of man should have risen from the dead*' (9.2–9, at v. 9). When the Marcan John the

Baptist prophesies that the Coming One 'will baptize you with the Holy Spirit' (1.8b), he does not have in mind a Lucan Pentecost.[57] Rather, the Spirit spoken of is the One who drives Jesus into the wilderness to be tested (1.12–13), and who will speak through persecuted believers when they are brought to trial (13.11); and the baptism spoken of is the baptism unto death (10.38–40). Intimations of glory are restricted severely. What dominates is the hard reality of the suffering of the Son of Man.

This is meat, not milk (cf. 1 Cor. 3.2). It is a spirituality for martyrs.[58] The question it raises must be: *Is Marcan spirituality so strenuous, so unremittingly dark, as to be oppressive?* Should Mark's gospel have a health warning attached to it? There may be something in this. Certainly, we should be a little more sanguine about the rather glib idea that the 'gospel' is inevitably 'good news'! But a number of points can be made in defence of Mark.

First, there is the *historical* point to do with the identity of Mark's audience. Perhaps Mark so accentuates the suffering of the Son of Man and the *theologia crucis*, because the people for whom he is writing have erred too far in the other direction, the direction of a *theologia gloriae* focused on an exalted Son of God who, in his earthly life, was a miracle-working 'divine man' (*theios aner*).[59] Perhaps, in other words, Mark's writing has a polemical side and a corrective bias which help to explain both its sharp cutting edge and its almost paranoid intensity. More likely, in my view, however, is the possibility that Mark is writing for 'fallible followers':[60] ordinary men and women who are followers of Jesus now risen, who find themselves in situations of persecution and oppression and whose resolve needs strengthening lest they lose heart and faith and 'fall away'. For such as these, the story of the suffering Son of Man who will come again in glory is presented as both theodicy ('the Son of man *must* suffer') and as example ('follow me').

As well as the historical point, there is the *canonical* point. Mark comes in the canon after Matthew. Perhaps, from the point of view of Christian spirituality, that is appropriate. Read in sequence, we move from a gospel of certainties, evidences, proofs, instructive discourses and Christian casuistry to a gospel where the blinding light of certainty is weaker, the evidences less watertight, the proofs more 'hermetic',[61] the discourses more opaque, and the casuistry almost nonexistent. Matthew is more easily digestible—though still demanding enough!—and provides more supports for those just learning (or relearning) to walk in the spiritual life. Mark, on the other hand, is for those forced by the stormy circumstances of life, and especially experiences of loss, to find stronger nourishment, stand on their own feet, and walk alongside others who have come that way too. It seems to me not at all surprising, therefore, that whereas Matthew ends with Jesus' promise of his ever-abiding *presence* (Matt. 28.20), Mark ends with the *absence* of Jesus (Mark 16:6) qualified by the mysterious announcement of the messenger that the Risen One 'goes before' his followers to Galilee.[62] This absence, this abrupt ending, is disturbing and challenging. It leaves the completion of the story open and lacking in clear definition. It leaves it to be filled out and acted out by every reader and listener prepared to take up the call to follow the Master wherever he leads.

Notes

1. Leslie Houlden, in *Ethics and the New Testament* (London: Mowbray, 1973), p. 48, puts it this way: 'With Matthew it is possible to speak of Christianity as a way of life and a path of duty. Jesus is not, as in Mark, the enigmatic Son of Man who is the source of a hard and mysterious way marked by the Cross (e.g. Mark viii, 34; x,38) so much as the authoritative teacher of clear and strenuous moral lessons . . . It is a shift from theology to Church law.'
2. Cf. A. Verhey, *The Great Reversal: Ethics and the New Testament* (Grand Rapids: Eerdmans, 1984), p. 78: 'However, the very assumption that Mark devotes very little of his Gospel to moral teaching needs to be challenged. The focus is . . . on heroic discipleship, but the major premise of discipleship makes the whole narrative a form of moral exhortation.'
3. For one other writer's attempt, see W.G. Thompson, *The Gospels for your Whole Life: Mark and John in Prayer and Study* (Minneapolis: Winston, 1983).
4. See further, J.R. Donahue, 'A Neglected Factor in the Theology of Mark', *Journal of Biblical Literature*, 101 (1982), pp. 563–94.
5. Cf. L.W. Hurtado, *One God, One Lord: Early Christian Devotion and Ancient Jewish Monotheism* (Philadelphia: Fortress, 1988).
6. So Donahue, 'Neglected Factor', p. 566 ff.. Exceptions are 9.37; 11.25; 12.27. Also, God is (to be) addressed as 'Father' in prayer, at 11.25; 14.36.

THE SPIRITUALITY OF MARK

7. My trans.: compare RSV of v. 33b: '. . . For you are not on the side of God, but of men.'

8. Cf. Donahue, 'Neglected Factor', pp. 581–2: 'Jesus speaks the language of a Hellenistic missionary preacher giving a proper interpretation of Judaism. . . . Jesus in effect teaches that belief in the one God and service of him is the foundation of any further belief.'

9. See further, B.M.F. van Iersel, 'The gospel according to St. Mark—written for a persecuted community?', *Nederlands Theologisch Tijdschrift*, 34 (1980), pp. 15–36.

10. Cf. H. Graham, 'A Passion Prediction for Mark's Community: Mark 13:9–13', *Biblical Theology Bulletin*, XVI (1986), pp. 18–22.

11. Cf. also, J. Marcus, 'Mark 4:10–12 and Marcan Epistemology', *Journal of Biblical Literature*, 103 (1984), pp. 557–74.

12. On the epiphanic language of fear, amazement, silence, trembling, etc., used in Mark to describe reactions to Jesus, see D.R. Catchpole, 'The Fearful Silence of the Women at the Tomb: A Study in Marcan Theology', *Journal of Theology for Southern Africa*, 18 (1977), pp. 3–10.

13. See further, P.J. Achtemeier, 'He Taught Them Many Things: Reflections on Marcan Christology', *Catholic Biblical Quarterly*, 42 (1980), pp. 465–81; and R.T. France, 'Mark and the Teaching of Jesus', in R.T. France and D. Wenham, eds., *Gospel Perspectives*, vol. 1 (Sheffield: JSOT, 1980), pp. 101–36.

14. Cf. also 1.21–22, 27; 2.13; 6.2, 6b, 34b; 8.31; 9.31; 10.1; 11.17–18; 12.14, 35, 38; 14.49. According to Achtemeier, 'Reflections', p. 474, *didaskein* consistently occurs in Mark's own editorial compositions, either introducing pieces of tradition or in summary statements: '. . . Mark has made certain that his readers gain the impression that whatever else Jesus did, he was engaged in regular activity as teacher.'

15. Cf. 4.38; 5.35; 9.17, 38; 10.17, 20, 35; 12.14, 19, 32; 13.1; 14.14. Note also addresses to Jesus as 'rabbi', in 9.5; 10.51; 11.21; 14.45.

16. Cf. Achtemeier, 'Reflections', p. 476–481, who shows, with special reference to the way healing miracles and teaching are combined inextricably, in 1.21–8 and 2.1–12, that the miracles function also to provide empirical verification of the power of Jesus' teaching: 'If the same power present in the mighty acts is present when Jesus teaches, a clear inference from the story in 1:21–27, then whenever he teaches, that power is present.'

17. See further, E. Best, *Following Jesus: Discipleship in the Gospel of Mark* (Sheffield: JSOT, 1981), Part 1.

18. So, too, Achtemeier, 'Reflections', p. 470.

19. Best, *Following Jesus*, p. 64.

20. See Best, *Following Jesus*, pp. 66–7.

21. See further, Best, *Following Jesus*, pp. 75–98.

22. Or does Mark have literal children in mind? The use of *enag-kalisamenos* in v. 36 suggests that the child is to be taken literally. On the other hand, the overall context of teaching for disciples 'on the way', and the specific appeal to the *shaliach* principle in v. 37, imply that the child is a metaphor of the missionary disciple. Note also that *dechesthai* ('to receive'), in v. 37 (4 times), is used of missionaries in 6.11. The evidence is set out in Best, *Following Jesus*, p. 78ff..

23. Best, *Following Jesus*, p. 83.

24. Houlden, *Ethics*, p. 44.

25. Cf. Verhey, *Reversal*, p. 79f., a section on Mark entitled, 'An Ethic of Freedom'.

26. Verhey, *Reversal*, p. 79.

27. See further, Best, *Following Jesus*, pp. 213–25.

28. Cf. F.J. Matera, *Passion Narratives and Gospel Theologies* (New York: Paulist Press, 1986), p. 68: 'By refusing to allow anyone to carry the instruments of worship through the temple, Jesus effectively calls a halt to the temple cult. With Jesus' death and the tearing of the temple curtain, the function of the temple, in Mark's view, comes to an end.'

29. On Marcan redaction in 11.17a, 18, see Best, *Following Jesus*, p. 217.

30. Cf. E.S. Malbon, *Narrative Space and Mythic Meaning in Mark* (New York: Harper & Row, 1986), p. 109: 'At 14:49 Jesus, in referring to his previous teaching in the temple . . . speaks as one who has rejected the temple and who is at the moment he speaks being arrested by its officials. At his passion Jesus dissociates himself from Jewish devotion to the temple. . . . At the death of Jesus the Jewish *naos* loses its function.'

31. See further, W.R. Telford, *The Barren Temple and the Withered Tree* (Sheffield: JSOT, 1980).

32. Although in 14.58 (cf.15.29) it is *false* witnesses who accuse Jesus of saying that he would destroy the temple and build another in three days, we should probably read this as an example of Marcan irony: those who are false saying what is true in spite of themselves. So, too, Matera, *Passion Narratives*, p. 68.

33. Cf. Houlden, *Ethics*, p. 45, speaking of Mark, says: 'For this writer . . . settling moral problems, in the everyday sense, was not a primary concern. He had no eye for casuistry. . . . [The explanation] is most likely to lie in his eschatology. For Mark, the End, though not immediately to appear (xiii, 7), was not far away.'

34. Cf. Achtemeier, 'Reflections', p. 469: 'The editorial point of the discourse seems to be advice to remain alert to the impending parousia (e.g. 13:8b, 13b, 23, 35a) . . .'

35. F. Kermode, *The Sense of an Ending* (London: Oxford University Press, 1966).

36. Verhey, *Reversal*, p. 79.
37. Cf. R.H. Lightfoot, *The Gospel Message of Mark* (Oxford: Clarendon Press, 1950), p. 48ff., noting p. 55: 'The arrival of the hour, the Lord's Passion, and the sufferings and endurance of His Church are linked indissolubly together.'
38. Note especially the essay of E. Schweizer, 'Mark's Theological Achievement', in W. Telford, ed., *The Interpretation of Mark* (London: SPCK, 1985), pp. 42–63, which deals successively with the blindness of the Pharisees, the blindness of the world, and the blindness of the disciples.
39. See J. Drury, 'Mark 1.1–15: An Interpretation', in A.E. Harvey, ed., *Alternative Approaches to New Testament Study* (London: SCM Press, 1985), p. 29ff..
40. Think especially of the story of the sacrifice of Isaac, noting Gen.22:1—After these things God tested Abraham . . .'.
41. I have explored this theme further in *Discipleship and Family Ties According to Mark and Matthew* (Ph.D. thesis, King's College London, 1991; forthcoming, Cambridge University Press).
42. Cf. E. Schweizer, 'The Portrayal of the Life of Faith in the Gospel of Mark', in J.L. Mays, ed., *Interpreting the Gospels* (Philadelphia: Fortress, 1981), pp. 168–182, esp. p. 170ff.; also, Best, *Following Jesus*.
43. Cf. W.M. Swartley, 'The Structural Function of the Term "Way" (*Hodos*) in Mark's Gospel', in W. Klassen, ed., *The New Way of Jesus* (Kansas: Faith and Life, 1980), pp. 73–86.
44. On which, see further, Catchpole, 'Silence'.
45. This is the burden of Malbon, *Narrative Space*.
46. Cf. also, 1.32–4, 45; 2.1ff.; 3.20, 32; 5.21; 6.30–44; etc.
47. Cf. D. Rhoads and D. Michie, *Mark as Story* (Philadelphia: Fortress, 1982), pp. 129–36.
48. See now, J.D. Kingsbury, *Conflict in the Gospel of Mark* (Philadelphia: Fortress, 1990).
49. I am accepting *orgistheis* as the original, omitted by Matthew and Luke. See the discussion in B.M. Metzger, *A Textual Commentary on the Greek New Testament* (London: United Bible Societies, 1971), *ad loc*.
50. See further, S.C. Barton, 'Mark as Narrative: The Story of the Anointing Woman (Mk 14:3–9)', *Expository Times*, 102/8 (1991), pp. 230–4.
51. See further, G. Twelftree, *Christ Triumphant: Exorcism Then and Now* (London: Hodder & Stoughton, 1985), pp. 116–122.
52. W.H. Vanstone, *The Stature of Waiting* (London: Darton, Longman & Todd, 1982), p. 5ff..
53. Vanstone, *Stature*, pp. 17–23.
54. Cf. W. Morrice, *Joy in the New Testament* (Grand Rapids: Eerdmans, 1985), pp. 91–104.

55. Cf. R.C. Tannehill, 'The Disciples in Mark: The Function of a Narrative Role', in W. Telford, ed., *The Interpretation of Mark* (London: SPCK, 1985), pp. 134–57, at p. 151: 'The disciples' story has come to a disastrous conclusion, and the author has spared nothing in emphasizing the disaster. This ending sends reverberations back through the whole preceding story.'

56. Surprisingly, Morna Hooker misses this point, in the chapter on 'Signs and Wonders', in *The Message of Mark* (London: Epworth Press, 1983), pp. 34–50.

57. So, too, R.A. Guelich, *Mark 1–8:26* (Dallas: Word Books, 1989), p. 25: 'The evangelist did not intend for the baptism with the Holy Spirit to be read through the Lukan eyes of Acts. . . . We have no hint of his bestowing the Spirit as a gift of power on his followers.'

58. See further, G.W.H. Lampe, 'St. Peter's Denial', *Bulletin of the John Rylands Library*, 55 (1972–3), pp. 346–368.

59. Cf. T.J. Weeden, *Mark—Traditions in Conflict* (Philadelphia: Fortress, 1971).

60. Cf. E.S. Malbon, 'Fallible Followers: Women and Men in the Gospel of Mark', in M.A. Tolbert, ed., *The Bible and Feminist Hermeneutics = SEMEIA*, 28 (1983), pp. 29–48.

61. Cf. F. Kermode, *The Genesis of Secrecy* (Cambridge, Mass.: Harvard University Press, 1979), for this line of approach.

62. So, too, Schweizer, 'Life of Faith', p. 180: 'The time after Easter is, for Mark, a time without Jesus. Nowhere does the Second Gospel speak of the exalted Lord in his church . . . Does not something of this unavailability of Jesus run throughout his teaching also?'

3
'You will have joy and gladness'

THE SPIRITUALITY OF LUKE-ACTS

Introduction

There can be no doubt that it is appropriate to engage in an inquiry into the spirituality of Luke-Acts. If by 'Christian spirituality' we mean learning the way of God revealed in Christ, then we find in Luke's two volumes a narrative record of the lives of the founder and first apostles of the Christian 'Way'. If spirituality is about life in the Spirit, then we could hardly do better than to study a work so frequently punctuated by accounts of manifestations of the Spirit's presence. If spirituality is about the spiritual life, then none of the gospels has more to say about prayer than Luke, none places greater emphasis on the importance of repentance, and none gives comparable attention to the qualities of character which the spiritual life requires. What is more, Luke is the first of the early Christian authors to have given us an account of the work of the Spirit after the departure of Jesus. In so doing, he gives us his vision of what the life of faith involves for the people of God in the period after the resurrection and ascension.

The discussion which follows is intended to focus primarily upon Luke's gospel. Our overall subject is, after all, the spirituality of the gospels. Nevertheless, points where what we find in the gospel is developed further in Acts will be noted, as well as any shifts of emphasis, in order both to reinforce the main points and also to show that Luke believed there to be a very substantial continuity between the period of Jesus and the period of the church.[1]

The spirituality of Luke-Acts described

1. In common with all the gospels, and with the New Testament as a whole, spirituality according to Luke begins with God and

what God has done in Christ. In other words, it is *a response to divine grace revealed in Christ*. It is impossible to separate Christian spirituality from theology and christology, and to talk about it just as a way of life. That would be a serious distortion, for it would have the effect of reducing spirituality to matters of morals. Not that Luke is uninterested in morality and other issues of a quite everyday kind, as we shall see. The fount and well-spring of what he has to say in these areas is not an ethical or philosophical tradition, however, but the story of Jesus and Christian origins rooted in the story of Israel, an extended narrative which is itself revelatory of the mighty acts of God for the salvation of the world. We will be unable to understand Lucan spirituality, therefore, unless we try to describe, however briefly, that revelation of divine grace to which it is a response.

First, then, Luke believes that *a new age has dawned*. This new age is the fulfilment of God's promises to his people Israel, the climax and culmination of all that has gone before. The idea of fulfilment is all-pervasive. 1.1 refers to other narratives of 'the things which have been accomplished among us'; it is said of John that he will go before the Lord 'in the spirit and power of Elijah' (1.17); the Magnificat ends by affirming of God that 'He has helped his servant Israel, in remembrance of his mercy, as he spoke to our fathers, to Abraham and to his posterity for ever' (1.54–5); and the Benedictus affirms, likewise, that the Lord God of Israel 'has visited and redeemed his people, and has raised up a horn of salvation for us in the house of his servant David, as he spoke by the mouth of his holy prophets from of old' (1.68ff.). Such evidence could be multiplied. Suffice it to add that Jesus' inaugural sermon in Nazareth proclaims the fulfilment, 'today', of the prophecy of Isaiah 61.1–2 (4.16ff.); and that the sermons of the apostles in Acts focus repeatedly upon the fulfilment of the divine plan prophesied beforehand in Scripture (e.g. Acts 2.14–36; 3.11–26, esp. v. 18; 7.1–53, esp. v. 52).

Second, Luke believes that *the new age has dawned with the births of John the Baptist and of Jesus*. That is why the birth and infancy narratives are given such prominence in Luke's first two chapters and why the birth of John and the birth of Jesus are interwoven so closely—a feature unique to this gospel. Just as John comes preparing the way of the Lord by his preaching and water baptism (3.1–20), and is subsequently superseded by Jesus (cf. 3.23ff.), so too at the outset, the birth of John prepares the way for, and is eclipsed by, the birth of the one who is greater, Jesus the divine Son (cf. 1.80 and 2.52). The import of this is that Luke's faith is thoroughly messianic: the new age has come with the births of the messiah (1.32–3, 68–79; cf. 2.4) and his forerunner (1.14–17).

Third, Luke believes that *the new age is the age of the eschatological Spirit*.[2] That is why both the miraculous births of John and Jesus at the beginning of the gospel and the birth of the church at the beginning of the Acts are marked by the activity of the Spirit.[3] These stories, together with the stories of miraculous deeds, powerful words, prophetic utterances and other charismatic manifestations in both volumes, express Luke's sense that the presence of God as Spirit is unmistakable in the events that have taken place. For Luke, God is not distant. He is present and reveals his will by means of messengers, both human and divine.[4] He is present in the person of his divine Son. And he is present in power at the end of the age as 'Holy Spirit'.

Fourth, Luke believes that *the new age is a time of salvation prior to the coming of the End*. In other words, the time of John and Jesus and subsequently of the church is a period of divine grace. Thus, Mary 'rejoices in God my *Saviour*' (1.47); John the Baptist will 'give knowledge of *salvation* to his people in the forgiveness of their sins' (1.77); the angel announces to the shepherds that, 'to you is born this day in the city of David a *Saviour*, who is Christ the Lord' (2.11); and Peter at Pentecost quotes the prophet Joel that, 'whoever calls on the name of the Lord *shall be saved*' (2.21), and in consequence of his testimony, 'the Lord added to their number day by day *those who were being saved*' (2.47). Typical also of Luke's strong emphasis on salvation is his use of *sozein* ('save') and cognates in many of the miracle stories (e.g. 6.9; 7.50; 8.36, 48, 50; 17.19; 18.42; cf. Acts 4.9, 12; 14.9; 27.20, 31), and in the speeches of the apostles (e.g. Acts 4.12; 11.14; 15.11; 16.30–1). Likewise, the culmination of the uniquely Lucan story of Zacchaeus is the double saying of Jesus: 'Today, salvation (*soteria*) has come to this house, since he also is a son of Abraham. For the Son of man came to seek and to save (*sosai*) the lost' (19.9).

Fifth, and finally, Luke believes that *the new age is a time of salvation for all people, that the grace of God is unrestricted*.

73

Thus, if John is significant primarily for his testimony to Israel (1.80), Jesus' significance is universal (2.52; cf. 3.1ff.). If Luke's first volume tells of the ministry of Jesus primarily to Israel and of his rejection by Israel, the second volume tells of what he *continued* to do (cf. Acts 1.1) through the Spirit-filled apostles— namely, mission to all nations. If Luke's first volume begins and ends in the temple of Jerusalem, his second begins in Jerusalem and ends in Rome, the capital of the empire. But it is not just Gentiles who are included within the scope of God's grace. For Luke, the gospel is good news for 'the poor' (cf. 4.18), an all-embracing term for all who recognize their need of God's help: the impoverished, the social outcast, the ill and diseased, those oppressed by virtue of their gender, social status, occupation, nationality, and so on. The words of the Nunc Dimittis express the universal scope of the divine grace, in a nutshell: 'Lord, now lettest thou thy servant depart in peace, according to thy word; for mine eyes have seen thy salvation which thou hast prepared in the presence of all peoples, a light for revelation to the Gentiles, and for glory to thy people Israel' (2.29–32).

2. I have tried in the foregoing to express the essential features of Luke's understanding of the revelation of divine grace in Christ. Now it is appropriate to describe *the kinds of response to grace* which go to make up what we may fairly call Lucan spirituality. There are seven major elements to which I wish to draw attention.

One of the most distinctive aspects of Lucan spirituality is *joy*. The inauguration of the new age of the eschatological Spirit with the coming of the messiah prompts a response of profound gratitude to God and optimism for the future which expresses itself in numerous outbursts of rejoicing. So dominant is this mood in Luke that his gospel has become known as 'the gospel of joy'. William Morrice points out the statistical basis for this: 'Of the 326 instances of words for joy in the New Testament, 53 occur within these 24 chapters. In addition, words for joy appear 26 times in the Acts of the Apostles. Thus, 24% of the New Testament vocabulary for joy is contained within the writings of Luke.'[5] Moving to the narrative itself, we note the following remarkable aspects of Luke's use of this motif.

First, the note of joy dominates the birth stories. The angel of the Lord tells Zechariah that 'you will have joy (*chara*) and gladness (*agalliasis*), and many will rejoice (*charesontai*)' at the birth of a son to the barren Elizabeth (1.14). When Elizabeth is greeted by Mary, we are told, first by the narrator, that 'the babe leaped (*eskirtesen*) in her womb' (1.41); and this is confirmed,and reinforced by Elizabeth herself, who says, 'the babe in my womb leaped for joy (*eskirtesen en agalliasei*)' (1.44). In the New Testament, the verb *skirtan* ('to leap') occurs only in Luke: in the two occurrences mentioned already, and in 6.23, as part of the final beatitude.[6] Clearly, for Luke, joy is something to be shared. It is an essential form of testimony to the experience of God's blessing. Hence, when John is born to Elizabeth, 'her neighbours and kinsfolk heard that the Lord had shown great mercy to her, and they rejoiced with her' (1.58). Even more so, the great canticles of Luke's first two chapters are classic testimonies to the joy which God's mercy calls forth. Mary, in the Magnificat, proclaims, 'My spirit rejoices (*egalliasen*) in God my Saviour' (1.47); Zechariah blesses God in the words of the Benedictus (1.68ff.; cf. v. 64); Simeon blesses God in the words of the Nunc Dimittis (2.28ff.); and Anna the prophetess praises (*anthomologein*—only here in the New Testament) God and speaks about Jesus to all 'who were looking for the redemption of Jerusalem' (2.38). Finally, no episode captures better the mood of joy at the birth of the messiah than the story of the shepherds (2.8–20). To these archetypal 'poor', a massive revelation is given: an angel of the Lord appears and 'the glory of the Lord' shines about them, and the angel announces, 'Be not afraid, for behold, I bring you good news of great joy (*charan megalen*) which will come to all the people . . .' (2.10). There follows suddenly the manifestation of the angelic host 'praising (*ainounton*) God' (2.13–14); and, after the shepherds have been to see the new-born Messiah, they return 'glorifying and praising (*doxazontes kai ainountes*) God for all they had heard and seen' (2.20). The beginning of Luke's gospel is dominated by a mood of doxology: exultant joy in God for the revelation of his mercy in the births of the messiah and his forerunner.

The same mood characterizes the ending of Luke's gospel, as well. At the resurrection appearance to the eleven and their companions in Jerusalem, Luke says that they 'disbelieved for joy and wondered' (24.41). The possibility that the apostles' doubt might have arisen out of unbelief of a more explicit kind is played down in favour of the motif of joyous amazement. This motif occurs again in the final episode, that of the ascension. After Jesus is taken up into heaven, we are told that 'they returned to Jerusalem with great joy and were continually in the temple blessing (*eulogountes*) God' (24.52–3). So the mood of joy frames the whole gospel.

Nor is joy confined to beginnings and endings. In the body of the narrative, it is all-pervasive also. Most notably, joy in God is an aspect of the life of Jesus himself. According to 10.17ff., the return of the seventy 'with joy' from a successful mission of exorcizing, causes Jesus great joy: 'In that same hour he rejoiced in the Holy Spirit (*egalliasato to pneumati to hagio*) . . .' (10.21; Luke only—cf. Matt. 11.25a). Only in Luke, of all the gospels, is this quality of exultant joy attributed explicitly to Jesus. Not surprisingly, therefore, Jesus teaches about joy, as well (cf. 10.20); and the famous parables of Jesus in Luke all culminate on this note. In Luke's version of the parable of the lost sheep (15.1–7 par. Matt. 18.12–14), the shepherd returns 'rejoicing' (v. 5) and calls together his friends and neighbours to 'Rejoice with me' (v. 6); and Jesus' comment is about the great 'joy in heaven' over the repentant sinner (v. 7). Exactly the same pattern recurs in the parable of the lost coin (15.8–10). Likewise, in the parable of the lost son (15.11–32), the imagery and terminology of festive joy at the return of the penitent prodigal are overwhelming. The verb *euphrainesthai* ('to be merry') occurs no fewer than four times (vv. 23, 24, 29, 32); and the concluding reproof to the elder brother combines *euphrainesthai* and *chairesthai* in a quite emphatic manner: 'It was fitting *to make merry and be glad*, for this your brother was dead and is alive; he was lost, and is found' (v. 32).

We can but conclude that joy is a fundamental aspect of Christian spirituality, according to Luke, in a way that distinguishes Lucan spirituality from that of the other evangelists. His emphasis on joy is unparalleled. Possible reasons for this emphasis are several. Perhaps it is a reaction to what he finds in his sources, and to Mark, in particular, where the unremitting shadow cast by that evangelist's *theologia crucis* allows little scope for glimpses of the light beyond, let alone of light and joyful hope in the present moment. Perhaps it is a reflection of Luke's own experience of the life of faith among the Spirit-filled people of God. For joy, in Luke's narrative, is not limited to the time of Jesus' earthly ministry: it is a feature of the life of the church and the Christian mission, too. Witness the cameo portrait of the *koïnonia* at Jerusalem, where Luke says that 'they partook of food with glad and generous hearts' (Acts 2.46). Witness also the joy in Samaria which greets the preaching and healing ministry of the apostle Philip (Acts 8.4–8, at v. 8), and the rejoicing of numerous converts upon their initiation into the Christian way (e.g. Acts 8.39; 13.48, 52; 16.34; cf. 15.3). It is not impossible that Luke focuses attention on the mood of joy, even joy in adversity (cf. Luke 6.22–3; Acts 5.41), because it chimes in with his own Christian experience. Be that as it may, it is clear also that Luke focuses on joy because of the way it functions theologically to highlight and reinforce his fundamental claim that the coming of Jesus is 'good news to the poor', the eschatological culmination of the mighty acts of God for the salvation of the world.[7]

A second major aspect of Lucan spirituality understood as a response to grace, is *repentance and conversion*. There can be no doubt that these are of prime importance to Luke. *Metanoia* ('repentance') and *metanoein* ('to repent') occur fourteen times in the gospel and eleven times in Acts; and this is almost half of the total for the New Testament as a whole.[8] In Luke's redaction of the story of the call of Levi (5.27–32 par. Mark 2.13–17), it is significant that where Mark has, 'I came not to call the righteous, but sinners', Luke adds, 'to repentance (*eis metanoian*)'. Jesus may be the 'friend of tax collectors and sinners' (7.34 par. Matt. 11.19), but only on condition of their repentance! Taking the two volumes as a whole, Brian Beck rightly points out that, 'For Luke, "repentance and forgiveness" together sum up the Christian good news'.[9] The evidence he cites bears this out. Jesus' parting words to the apostles, prior to his departure, are a reminder 'that repentance and forgiveness of sins should be preached in his name to all nations' (24.47); and in the speeches of the apostles in Acts, the constant refrain is the call to repentance for the forgiveness of sins (e.g. 2.38; 3.19; 5.31; 8.22).

Closely related to repentance is conversion.[10] The only occurrence of *epistrophe* ('conversion') in the New Testament comes in Acts 15.3, which tells of the journey of Paul and Barnabas through Phoenicia and Samaria, 'reporting the conversion of the Gentiles'. *Epistrepsein* ('to turn around', 'to convert') is more frequent in the New Testament, but by far the majority of uses (eighteen in all) come in Luke-Acts. Of John it is prophesied that 'he will turn (*epistrepsei*) many of the sons of Israel to the Lord their God' (1.16; cf. v. 17). To Peter, at the end of the gospel, Jesus says, in respect of the denial, 'and when you have turned again (*epistrepsas*), strengthen your brethren' (22.32). And in the speeches in Acts, the summons to 'turn around', in the sense of 'convert', is especially dominant. Typical are the words of Peter, in Acts 3.19: 'Repent, therefore, and turn again (*epistrepsate*), that your sins may be blotted out, that times of refreshing may come from the presence of the Lord' (cf. also 9.35; 11.21; 14.15; 15.19; 26.18, 20; 28.27).

To get a clearer idea of what is involved in repentance and conversion, we can do no better, however, than focus on the conversion stories which punctuate Luke-Acts. In the gospel, classic instances are the story of the woman with the ointment (7.36–50), the parable of the lost son (15.11–32), the story of Zacchaeus (19.1–10), and the story of the penitent thief (23.39–43). The story of the woman with the ointment is traditional (cf. Mark 14.3–9; Matt. 26.6–13; John 12:1–8), but Luke has interpreted it quite distinctively.[11] In Mark, for example, it has a different setting in both time and place. Coming at the opening of Mark's passion narrative, it serves to express the meaning of discipleship of the crucified one. Luke, by contrast, sets the event in the early part of Jesus' ministry, in Galilee, and locates the story in the house of a different Simon, Simon the Pharisee. For Luke, the story is not a passion story but a story of repentance, conversion and salvation, where salvation comes, strikingly, not to the Pharisee host, but to 'a woman of the city, who was a sinner' (7.37a). In the Lucan context, the story expresses the soteriological claim of the immediately preceding discourse (7.24–35): that Jesus the Son of Man is 'a friend of tax collectors and sinners'[12] and that it is people such as these who are the children of Wisdom (i.e. God) and who 'justify' God (7.35) by their repentance and faith. The

dynamic of the story expresses supremely well Luke's understanding of the dynamic of repentance and salvation. The woman
learns of Jesus' presence in the Pharisee's house and comes
seeking him out. In humility, she stands behind him at his feet;
in remorse for her sins, she weeps (cf. 22.62), something which
recalls the reader to the third beatitude (6.21b); and in a spirit
of humble repentance and deep devotion, she washes his feet
with her tears, wipes them with her hair, kisses them, and anoints
them with ointment (7.37–8). Notably, she says not a word. Her
actions and emotions speak for themselves. And Jesus, in
controverting the unbelieving and self-righteous Pharisee, confirms her in her enacted faith. According to Jesus, it is she who
has shown true hospitality to him, not Simon (7.44–6): it is she
who has 'loved much' (7.47). At the end, therefore, Jesus' final
words are for her: 'Your faith has saved you; go in peace' (7.50).
Not by coincidence, furthermore, is this episode succeeded by
the Lucan seam at 8.1–3, where the narrator tells of Jesus
continuing his journey, 'preaching and bringing the good news
of the kingdom of God', and having in his company, not only the
twelve apostles, but also many women 'who provided for them
out of their means'. For Luke, the good news to the poor is good
news to women also, and many of them respond, like the
penitent prostitute, by becoming followers of Jesus.[13]

   In the parable of the lost son,[14] the prodigal is a sinner too: he
dishonours his father by treating him as if he were dead, he
squanders his property in 'loose living', and he associates with
Gentiles, even accepting employment as a swineherd. By virtue
of his imprudence and selfish extravagance, he impoverishes
himself and places himself beyond the pale, geographically,
socially, economically and religiously. He is truly 'lost'. In Lucan
terms, he is one of 'the poor'. But there comes a turning-point.
The son 'comes to himself' (15.17a), returns to his father, and in
humility confesses, 'I have sinned against heaven and before you'
(15.21, a repetition of v. 18!). Of course, the parable is as much
about the compassionate love of the father as it is about the fall
and restoration of the son. It is a celebration, not only of
repentance, but also and at the same time, of forgiveness. The
second half of the parable takes up this very point. The elder
brother, by his self-righteous refusal to enter into the compassionate joy of the father at the return of the prodigal, shows that

he himself is lost and in need of that humility and change of heart which his younger brother had discovered. Repentance and conversion, therefore, are not just 'once and for all time' affairs: both the 'righteous' and the 'sinner', the insider and the outsider, need to repent in order to share in the joy of the divine bounty. Luke's warning to those among his readers with a disposition towards what Beck calls 'the Pharisaic mind'[15] is clear. It is made explicit at 16.14–15, unique to Luke: 'The Pharisees, who were lovers of money, heard all this, and they scoffed at him. But he said to them, "You are those who justify yourselves before men, *but God knows your hearts*; for what is exalted among men is an abomination in the sight of God"' (cf. 15.1–2).

The story of Zacchaeus is another classic conversion story unique to Luke (19.1–10). By virtue of its setting in Jericho, it is linked closely with the previous episode which Luke has drawn from the tradition, the story of the healing of the blind man (18.35–43 par. Mark 10.46–52). That story is a paradigm of conversion also, so that the two in sequence are mutually reinforcing.[16] The blind man, responding to the coming of Jesus, cries out to the Messiah for mercy, and persists in so doing in spite of opposition. Jesus, in turn, responds to the blind man by commanding that he be brought to him. When this is done, the blind man humbly confesses his need of healing, to which Jesus responds further, 'Receive your sight, your faith has saved (*sesoken*) you' (18.42, my trans.). Then, the blind man is healed, not only physically, but spiritually as well, for 'he followed him, glorifying God' with an eschatological joy which is chorused by 'all the people' (18.43). Similarly Zacchaeus. He too is impoverished, not by blindness, but by his occupation and wealth: 'he was a chief tax collector, and rich' (19.2; cf. 5.27–32). He too responds to the coming of Jesus, and overcomes the obstacles of the crowd and his small stature in order to see him. Remarkably, in an act of mercy and forgiveness, Jesus offers to go with him to his home. This precipitates Zacchaeus' conversion and repentance. Not only does he receive Jesus 'joyfully' (19.6); he also controverts Jesus' opponents by promising both sacrificial almsgiving to the poor and generous compensation to those whom he has cheated (19.8). Just as, in the previous episode, Jesus confirmed the blind man's conversion by pronouncing him 'saved', so too Jesus confirms Zacchaeus' conversion by saying, 'Today, salvation has come to this house' (19.9f.).

The 'today' (*semeron*) of Zacchaeus' salvation provides a natural link with our other example of a Lucan conversion story, that of the penitent criminal (23.39–43).[17] Here, Luke differs markedly from Mark and Matthew in that, where they have the two criminals crucified with Jesus both reviling him (Mark 15.32b par. Matt. 27.44), Luke draws a contrast between them, which is symbolized spatially in the detail that one is crucified on Jesus' right, the other on his left (23.33b; cf. John 19.18). One of the criminals—Luke uses the term, *kakourgoi*, 'evil-doers'—is said to 'blaspheme' Jesus, and reveals his impenitence and self-interest by saying to Jesus, 'Save yourself and us!'. In Luke, it is the unbelievers who tell Jesus to save himself: first, the rulers (23.35), then the soldiers (23.37), then the impenitent criminal (23.39). They cannot see that it is only by dying that Jesus is able to save. The other criminal responds quite differently, in penitence and faith. Having witnessed Jesus' spirit of forgiveness of his enemies (23.34a), he rebukes his fellow criminal for not 'fearing God', and points out that, whereas they are suffering the just penalty for their misdeeds, Jesus is innocent. This confession is followed by the prayer of faith in Jesus as messiah: 'Jesus, remember me when you come into your kingdom' (23.42, my trans.); to which Jesus responds with the words of assurance of salvation, 'Truly, I say to you, today you will be with me in Paradise' (23.43). No time is too late for confession of sin and repentance; and once again, even hanging on the cross, Jesus preaches good news to the poor, embodied, this time, in the person of a convicted criminal.

On the basis of stories of repentance and conversion such as these, we may summarize Luke's understanding thus. First, repentance is the only appropriate response to the dawn of the new age with the coming of the messiah, and is a prerequisite of forgiveness and salvation. Second, repentance involves a change of heart and issues in a change of life oriented on Jesus and the kingdom of God. Third, those most likely to repent and respond to the 'good news' of the gospel are 'the poor', those whose physical and spiritual circumstances render them receptive to the grace of God made known by his Son. Fourth, repentance and conversion have as their blessed accompaniment experiences or anticipations of eschatological joy, the focus of which (in some cases) is hospitality and the festive sharing of food.

If we ask why Luke should give such prominence to this theme, we need to allow for various possibilities. The most likely reason is that, for Luke, it is important, not only that the new age has dawned and that salvation is available, but also *to make clear how to appropriate it.* Perhaps Luke's readers needed not only an accurate and reassuring account of the mighty acts of God on which to build their faith, but also instruction and examples showing what was required in response. This might be particularly important for Gentile converts, not familiar with the strong biblical tradition of repentance and turning back to God which would be so well known to Jews. What Paul writes to the Gentile converts at Thessalonica provides a useful analogy. Here, Paul stresses the reality of their conversion, when he reminds them 'how you turned to God *(epestrepsate pros ton theon)* from idols, to serve a living and true God' (1 Thess. 1.9). But he also goes on to emphasize the requisite impact of this 'turning' on their lives, as mediated to them by the example of himself and his co-workers: 'You are witnesses, and God also, how holy and righteous and blameless was our behaviour to you believers; for you know how, like a father with his children, we exhorted each one of you . . . to lead a life worthy of God, who calls you into his own kingdom and glory' (1 Thess. 1.10–12).

Another possible reason why Luke so emphasizes repentance and conversion may be his sense that *there might be some among his readers who are taking their faith too lightly and not letting it affect their attitudes and lifestyles.* Maybe this is why Luke is so consistently hostile to 'the Pharisaic mind' with its complacency and self-righteousness.[18] In the Lucan characterization, Pharisees are people who refuse to repent (cf. 7.30). Because they are 'lovers of money' (16.14), like Dives in the parable (16.19–31), they are unable to repent even if someone should rise from the dead, a statement of particular poignance in the period after the resurrection of Jesus! Corresponding with their refusal to repent is their proneness to 'justify' *(dikaioun)* themselves before their fellows (16.15), an attitude explored in the Lucan parable of the Pharisee and the tax collector (18.10–14), the moral of which is made explicit at the outset: 'He also told this parable to some who trusted in themselves that they were righteous *(dikaioi)* and despised others.' The consequence of this proneness to self-justification is both that it blinds the Pharisee to his own sinfulness before God (who 'knows your hearts', 16.15), and that it renders him without the capacity to forgive—like the elder brother in the parable of the lost son, unable to forgive and therefore unable to share in the joy of his father at the prodigal's return (15.25–32). A corollary of this is the Pharisee's lack of compassion and indifference to human need: 'There is nothing about them of the spontaneity of generous love which marks the sermon on the plain or the parable of the Good Samaritan.'[19]

A third possible reason for Luke's emphasis on repentance and conversion also has to do with theology and spirituality: namely, that the stories of conversion allow Luke to represent *the universal scope of the divine mercy*. In the Gospel, as we have seen, those who repent and turn around include a streetwise prostitute, a rebellious and destitute son, a wealthy tax collector, and a crucified criminal. In the Acts, conversion stories are prominent too. Most striking, perhaps, is the attention given to the conversion of the centurion, Cornelius, and his household (Acts 10.1–11.18), and the story of Saul's conversion, which is told no fewer than three times (Acts 9.1–19; 22.1–16; 26.9–18).[20] The significance of the former story lies above all in the fact that Cornelius is a God-fearing Gentile, and of the latter in the fact that Saul is a Pharisee who persecutes the church but whom the risen Lord summons to mission to both Israel and the Gentiles. It is as if Luke is saying over and over, and in as many ways as possible, that God's grace and forgiving mercy are bounteous and unrestricted, and that no one, therefore, is beyond the pale unless they place themselves beyond.

We have drawn attention, so far, to joy and to repentance and conversion as important aspects of Lucan spirituality understood as response to the revelation of God's grace in Christ. A third major aspect is *faith*.[21] This is a close corollary of repentance and conversion, but, as we shall see, it is understood by Luke to be important for continuing in the Christian life, not just at the point of beginning.

First, however, faith (*pistis*) or believing (*pisteuein*) in Jesus is what conversion involves, and such faith brings salvation. As Paul says to the Philippian jailer: 'Believe (*pisteuson*) in the Lord

Jesus, and you will be saved, you and your household' (Acts 16.31; cf. 15.11). In Acts as a whole, we note the following: Christians are termed, 'those who believed (*hoi pisteuontes*)' (Acts 2.44; cf. 5.14; 15.5); believing takes place in response to hearing 'the word' (4.4; cf. 16.32) or the 'good news about the kingdom of God and the name of Christ' (8.12); it makes possible miracles of healing (3.16; cf. 14.9) or it may occur in response to the miraculous when interpreted by 'the teaching of the Lord' (13.12); it establishes a spiritual unity between believers (4.32— 'of one heart and soul'); it is open to both men and women (5.14; cf. 8.12; 17.12, 34), Jews and Greeks (14.1; cf. 14.27; 15.7, 9; 17.12; 20.21; 21.20, 25; 26.18); it opens the way to being baptized (8.12, 13; cf. 16.33; 18.8); it brings forgiveness of sins (10.43; cf. 26.18); it is associated with receiving the Holy Spirit (11.15–17; cf. 6.5; 11.24; 19.1–7); it involves 'turning' to the Lord (11.21; cf. 19.18–20; 26.18); it brings a freedom greater than that made possible by law-observance (13.39); it is an act made possible by divine grace (13.48b; cf. 27.25); it brings joy to the believer (16.34b); and it is understood to be grounded in the scriptures and the faith of Israel (24.14; cf. 26.27). Such a catalogue shows how important faith or believing is for Luke's understanding of salvation and entry into the Christian way. As Beck puts it: conversion 'is an act of believing, not just of renunciation or the adoption of a new lifestyle or identification with a new community'.[22]

Intimations of the same come also in Luke's gospel. For instance, in Luke's version of the interpretation of the parable of the sower, the first category of hearers of the word do not come to the point of conversion, because the devil 'takes away the word from their hearts, *that they may not believe and be saved*' (Luke 8.12; diff. Mark and Matt.). Here, Luke has introduced *pistis* terminology in order to highlight how important faith is for salvation. Similarly, at 8.50 (cf. 8.48), Luke makes explicit that faith is a prerequisite for healing-as-salvation. Says Jesus to Jairus: 'Only believe (*pisteuson*, aorist imperative), and she shall be saved (*kai sothesetai*).'[23] The same point is made in the uniquely Lucan story of the healing of the ten lepers (17.11– 19, at v.19); but in addition, attention is drawn most emphatically to the fact that the one who shows faith by praising God and turning back to give thanks to Jesus, is a Samaritan, a 'foreigner (*allogenes*)' (17.16b, 18). He is like the Gentile centurion earlier on who is also singled out by Jesus on account of his faith (7.9 par. Matt. 8.10). At the trial, it is only the Lucan Jesus who replies to the Sanhedrin, 'If I tell you, you will not believe . . .' (22.67). Finally, on the Emmaus road, the two disciples are rebuked for being 'slow of heart to believe (*pisteuein*) all that the prophets have spoken' (24.25, Luke only). We can conclude with confidence, therefore, that 'the act of believing' is as fundamental to salvation in the gospel as it is in the Acts.

But faith is required for salvation, not just at the outset, but all along the way. It is a matter, not just of 'momentary, decisive response',[24] but of continuous commitment. Indicative of this is the way in which Luke can use the perfect participal form, *hoi pepisteukotes* (lit. 'those who have come to believe and continue to do so') to describe Christians, in the Acts (e.g. 15.5; 18.27; 19.18; 21.20, 25). We note also, that the expression 'the faith' (*he pistis*) is used as a description of the life of Christian discipleship: as at Acts 14.22, where Paul and Barnabas retrace their steps through several cities, exhorting the new converts 'to continue in the faith (*emmenein tei pistei*), and saying that through many tribulations we must enter the kingdom of God' (cf. 6.7; 13.8; 16.5).

This idea of faith as something demanding persistence and continual strengthening occurs in the gospel, as well. Returning to the interpretation of the parable of the sower (Luke 8.11–15),[25] we note that the second category is made up of those who '*believe for a while*' (8.13b; diff. Mark and Matt., which have '*endure* for a while'), but fall away in time of temptation; the third is made up of those whose fruit 'does not mature (*ou telesphorousin*)' under the pressure of the cares and pleasures of life (8.14; diff. Mark and Matt.: 'it proves unfruitful [*akarpos*]'); and the fourth consists of those who, 'hearing the word, hold it fast in an honest and good heart, and bring forth fruit with patience' (8.15). Unlike Mark and Matthew, which focus at the end on the abundant yield of the seed in the good soil, Luke focuses on the fundamental importance of having a right heart (as a guard against hypocrisy), holding on tight to the received word, and bearing fruit 'with patience' (RSV) or, perhaps better, 'with perseverance (*en hupomone*)' (cf. 21.19).

Several other references cohere with this emphasis on faith as perseverance. One is the uniquely Lucan parable of the unjust judge (18.1–8), told in the context of teaching about the coming of the kingdom of God (17.20ff.). The parable reaches a climax with the question: 'Nevertheless, when the Son of man comes, will he find faith (*ten pistin*) on earth?' (18.8b). The meaning of 'faith', here, is given in the parable's introductory commentary by the evangelist: 'And he told them a parable, to the effect that they ought always to pray and not lose heart' (18.1). Faith, in other words, is about loyalty, and it demands perseverance: in this case, perseverance expressed through prayer. Similarly, another reference to faith, once more unique to Luke, where Jesus addresses the apostle Peter at the last supper: 'Simon, Simon, Satan demanded to have you, that he might sift you like wheat, but I have prayed for you that your faith may not fail . . .' (22.31–2). Again, faith is about persistent loyalty to Christ, especially through times of testing (cf. 8.25), and prayer is a means of sustaining that faith.

Why does Luke give such prominence to the theme of faith-as-perseverance in both volumes of his writing? First, and foremost, Luke is aware of *the danger of apostasy*. This danger threatens the believer in many forms. It may be Satan-inspired testing or temptation (cf. 4.1–13). As Jesus' words to Peter at the last supper show, Luke believes that the world is a realm where Satan is active: 'Satan demanded to have you . . .' (22.31; cf. 10.17–20). It may be the threat to the loyalty of faith posed by potentially competing loyalties; and here, Luke gives particular attention to wealth, business concerns and family ties (cf. 6.24–6; 8.14; 9.57–62; 10.38–42; 12.13–21; 14.15–24; 16.1–13, 19–31; 17.26ff.; etc.). It may be the threat posed by persecution from unbelievers (cf. 6.22–3, 27–8; 9.23–7; 12.49–53; 21.12–19; etc.). It may be that the eschatological hope of some is waning in view of the delay of the coming of the Son of Man (cf. 17.20–18.8; 21.8–11 [diff. Mark 13:5–8], 28; etc.). It may be the threat posed by the vacuum created by the deaths of the leading apostles of the first generation. Particularly revealing is Paul's lengthy farewell address to the elders of the church of Ephesus in Acts 20.17–38. Here, special emphasis is placed on: the fact of Paul's departure never to return; the need to beware of 'fierce wolves' coming in to create havoc among the Christian flock; the danger of false prophets leading people astray from within the fellowship; the necessity of continued trust in God and his word; and the importance of not coveting another's property and of generosity. The danger of apostasy is very real and threatens from many quarters. Luke's response, as we have seen, is to encourage a spirituality of joy, so that the dangers which threaten can be transcended; a spirituality of repentance and conversion, so that complacency and self-righteousness can be left behind; and a spirituality of faith, so that the present times of testing can be endured in full loyalty to God and his Christ.

The fourth major facet of Lucan spirituality which demands attention has surfaced already in what we had to say about faith. For we noted there that faith as a quality of continuing Christian existence is nurtured by, and expressed through, *prayer*. It is to prayer in Luke-Acts that we now turn.[26]

There can be no doubt of the importance of prayer in Luke's understanding of life lived in obedience to God. More than the other gospels, for example, Luke depicts Jesus as a person of prayer. On a number of crucial occasions, Luke edits his Marcan source in order to show Jesus as one who prays. Thus, at the baptism of Jesus, Luke has, 'and when Jesus also had been baptized *and was praying*, the heaven was opened . . .' (3.21; diff. Mark 1.9–10). The coming of the Holy Spirit upon Jesus is presented as a divine response to the obedience of Jesus in baptism and to his openness to God in prayer. This openness to God characterizes the Lucan Jesus from the very outset of his ministry.

The story of the call of the Twelve begins, in Luke's version alone, with the record that, 'And it came to pass in those days he went out to the mountain *to pray*, and he was all night *in prayer* to God' (6.12, my trans.; diff. Mark 3.13). In preparation for this next critical point in his ministry, the choosing of the twelve apostles, Jesus communes alone and apart with God throughout the night. So his choice is directed by God, and there is therefore (Luke implies) good reason to be confident in the witness of the ones chosen.

Luke's version of the great confession by Peter, which he sets, not at Caesarea Philippi, but in the context of an extended christological prelude (at 9.7–50) to his special travel narrative,[27] is distinctive once again in setting the episode in a context of

87

Jesus at prayer: 'Now it happened that *as he was praying alone* the disciples were with him; and he asked them, "Who do the people say that I am?"' (9.18; diff. Mark 8.27). It is as if Luke wants the reader to understand that Jesus' question to the disciples springs, not out of personal egotism on his part, but from the prayerful decision of Jesus that it is time for the disciples to learn that he, the Christ, is also the suffering Son of Man (cf. vv. 21–2).

Then there is the transfiguration (9.28–36 par. Mark 9.2–8). Here, in contrast to Mark, Luke says that Jesus 'took with him Peter and John and James, and went up on the mountain *to pray*. And *as he was praying*, the appearance of his countenance was altered, and his raiment became dazzling white' (9.28–9). Noteworthy here is the clear inference in Luke's version that the transfiguration occurs as a divine response to Jesus' communion with God in prayer. Luke wants the reader to recognize the profound depth of Jesus' relationship with God and the consequent power of his prayer. This episode is the high-point of the first part of Jesus' ministry, and it is marked out by a massive revelation of the divine presence in response to the prayerfulness of Jesus.

In addition to the places where Luke introduces the motif of Jesus at prayer into his Marcan source, there are other significant occurrences unique to Luke. In 10.21, with the successful return from mission of the seventy, Luke prefaces Jesus' prayer of thanksgiving to the Father by saying that Jesus 'rejoiced in the Holy Spirit (*egalliasato to pneumati to hagio*)' (diff. Matt. 11.25). Once more, Jesus' deep sense of the divine presence, here, of God's presence as Spirit, is plain. We are reminded that Jesus is the one upon whom the Spirit has come, in such tangible form, at his baptism (3.22).

Luke's version of the giving of the Lord's Prayer is set, not in the context of the sermon on the mount/plain, as is the case with Matthew's version, but in the more general context of Jesus, once again, at prayer: '*He was praying in* a certain place, and when he ceased, one of his disciples said to him, "Lord, teach us to pray, as John taught his disciples"' (11.1; diff. Matt. 6.9). Important here is the fact that the disciple's request for instruction in how to pray is a response to the example of Jesus praying. The spirituality of Jesus has a strong exemplary quality. Jesus' life of regular communion with God in prayer prompts in his disciple a desire to imitate him. Important also is the fact that Jesus' teaching on what to pray is extraordinarily short (vv. 2–4; cf. 20.47 par. Mark 12.40)! It is as if Luke's primary concern is to present Jesus as one who teaches about prayer by doing it, rather than by talking about it.

Only Luke has the two parables about prayer, known respectively as, the parable of the friend at midnight (11.5–8), and the parable of the unjust judge (18.1–8). Both of these parables have a similar point: the importance of persistence in prayer. Jesus' words to Peter at the last supper, 'I have prayed for you that your faith may not fail' (22.31–2), are important also. They show that Jesus' prayer involves, not only the 'vertical' dimension of communion with God, seeking God's will for his own life, but also the 'horizontal' dimension of prayer for his companions in their discipleship.

Luke's account of Jesus at prayer in Gethsemane is quite distinctive (22.40–6 par. Mark 14:32–42).[28] In Mark, the focus is both on Jesus' desolate sorrow as he wrestles repeatedly with God over the fate that awaits him, and on his bitter isolation due to the failure of his inner circle of disciples to remain awake and watch. In Luke, by contrast, the episode becomes a kind of prayer 'master class'! Thus, Luke tells us that Jesus went to the Mount of Olives, 'as was his custom (*kata to ethos*)' (22.39a), reinforcing the overall impression of the gospel that prayer is an habitual part of Jesus' life. His disciples 'follow' him (22.39b), with the implication that they will learn something. The lesson is imparted at the beginning and at the end: 'Pray that you may not enter into temptation' (22.40, 46b). All the disciples are present, not just Peter, James and John, so that all may learn from Jesus' example. Jesus does not fall on the ground in desperation, but in humility kneels to pray (v. 41).[29] Only once, not three times as in Mark, does he petition God to 'remove the cup', but even then he prefaces the petition with an 'if thou art willing' and follows it with, 'nevertheless not my will, but thine, be done' (v. 42). Jesus is the humble, obedient Son and the model of how to pray in testing times.

This brings us to the crucifixion (23.33ff.).[30] What we find in Luke's version is quite consistent with what we found in the Gethsemane story. Jesus does not die in sorrowful desolation, but in tranquil communion with the Father. Striking is the fact that, of the three (or four, if the 'loud cry' of v. 46a is distinguished from the prayer of v. 46b) sayings of Jesus from the cross, the first and last are prayers to the Father (vv. 34a, 46a) and the second is the promise of paradise to the penitent criminal (v. 43). The first prayer is a prayer in the spirit of the Lord's Prayer (cf. 11.2–4). It is addressed to God as 'Father', and it is a prayer for the forgiveness of those who have sinned against Jesus. The second is also addressed to God as 'Father', and is a prayer of trust, in the spirit of the psalmist (cf. Ps. 31.5). Jesus' prayer is exemplary to the last. Thus, both his prayers from the cross serve as the model for the prayers of the martyr Stephen, in Acts 7.59, 60. It is important to note also, that Jesus' entire public ministry is framed by depictions of him at prayer, from the baptism to the crucifixion.

The portrayal of Jesus as a person of prayer, habitually in deep communion with the Father, especially at points of moment or decision or testing in his life, and giving his disciples an example to follow, is an indelible part of Luke's gospel narrative. There can be no doubt that it is so because Luke wants to encourage in his readers also a spirituality of prayerfulness, of openness to God at all times. This way, a sense of the presence of God will grow, apostasy in time of temptation and trial will be avoided, and God will be able to guide his people unerringly along the Christian Way as he works out his saving purpose in history.

The portrayal of the apostles and of church life in the Acts reinforces this conclusion. Briefly, we may note the following. First, prayer features regularly in the accounts of the life of the church, from its very inception in the period following the ascension, onwards (e.g. 1.14; 2.42; 12.5; 14.23). As Trites points out, 'prayer was so characteristic of Christian discipleship that "calling upon his name" was often used as a synonymn (*sic*) to describe what is meant to be a Christian (2.21; 7.59; 9.14, 21; 22.16).'[31] Second, the apostles and leaders of the church are depicted, like Jesus, as people of prayer (e.g. 3.1; 8.15—Peter and John; 6.4—the Twelve; 7.59–60—Stephen; 10.9—Peter; 16.25—Paul and Silas; 20.36—Paul and the Ephesian elders). Third, the coming of the Holy Spirit to empower the church is depicted as a response to prayer (e.g. 2.1–13; 4.31; 8.15). Fourth, each new development or crisis in the life of the church comes in response to prayer or is negotiated with the help of prayer (e.g. 1.24ff.—the appointment of Matthias; 6.6—the appointment of the Seven; 7.59–60—Stephen, at his martyrdom; 8.14ff.—the coming of the Holy Spirit upon the Samaritan converts: 9.11; 22.17—the conversion of Saul; 10.2, 4, 30; 11.5—the conversion of the Gentile Cornelius; 13.2–3—the mission from Antioch). Fifth, women as well as men engage in prayer (e.g. 1.14; 12.12; 16.13; 21.5). Sixth, prayer brings deliverance of various kinds, such as physical healing (e.g. 9.40; 28.8), forgiveness (e.g. 7.60; 8.22), personal salvation (e.g. 8.24; 10.2, 30), and liberty from imprisonment (e.g. 12.12; 16.25ff.). Finally, prayer, thanksgiving and rejoicing are linked in a way which gives the church a strong doxological ethos (e.g. 2.46–7; 13.48; 27.35; 28.15).

Prayer, therefore, is kept constantly before the reader of Luke's two volumes. It is as characteristic of the apostolic church as it is of the Lord of the apostles. It is the means of communion with God in order that God's presence and Spirit may be experienced and in order that his will may be done. It is linked integrally with the other major aspects of Lucan spirituality we have covered so far, for it provides the channel for joy and thanksgiving, it provides the language for repentance and forgiveness, and it functions as the rich soil in which an enduring faith is able to grow.

It will be noticed, perhaps, that the aspects of Lucan spirituality to which I have drawn attention so far—joy, repentance and conversion, faith, and prayer—are predominantly 'vertical' in their orientation: that they have to do primarily with personal relations with God, with his Son Jesus, and with God's Spirit. In my view, this is entirely appropriate. The 'vertical' dimension *is* strong in Luke-Acts, after all, as the following evidence indicates.

There are angels which come and go from heaven and which fill the heavens with the praises of God. There are the powerful manifestations of the presence of the Holy Spirit, not least in the births of the messiah and his forerunner and in the birth of the church, as well as in miracle-working and in the effective ministry of the word. There are the occasions when the divine voice speaks from heaven or from out of a cloud. There are Jesus' visits to mountains to pray (6.12; 9.28, 37; 22.39). There are also, and most importantly for Luke, the accounts of the ascension, at which Jesus is 'carried up into heaven' (Luke 24.51).[32] The sense of the vertical is particularly strong in the opening chapters of the Acts narrative: 'until the day when he was taken up' (1.2, 22); 'as they were looking on, he was lifted up, and a cloud took him out of their sight' (1.9); 'as they were gazing into heaven' (1.10); 'Men of Galilee, why do you stand looking into heaven? This Jesus who was taken up from you into heaven, will come in the same way as you saw him go into heaven' (1.11); and, at the climax of Peter's Pentecost sermon, the emphasis on Jesus' exaltation 'at the right hand of God' (2.33, 34). This same 'vertical' orientation permeates Acts: Stephen is granted a vision of the open heaven revealing 'the glory of God and Jesus standing at the right hand of God' (7.55, 56); Saul is blinded by the light from heaven and receives a heavenly audition (9.3ff.); and Peter has a thrice-repeated vision of the heavens opening and a sheet of unclean animals descending and being taken up again (10.9–16).

It is with strong justification, therefore, that our description of Lucan spirituality should correlate with this strong 'vertical' orientation in Luke's narrative. Indeed, we need to take this correlation further still, by drawing attention to a fifth major aspect of Lucan spirituality: namely, *the sense of the presence of the exalted Lord*.[33] In Mark, the risen Christ is present mysteriously as the one who 'goes before' his disciples into 'Galilee'. In Matthew, Jesus promises to be with his disciples always, although how is not made clear: his word is meant to suffice. In John, there is the promise of the presence of 'another Paraclete'. Paul talks about being 'in Christ' and having 'Christ in you'. Such examples show that the early Christians all have a strong sense of the continuing vitality and presence of Christ, and that they represent that sense differently. Luke is no exception. More than his fellow synoptists, certainly, he emphasizes the absence of the Lord in heaven, at God's right hand. How, then, is he experienced as present to his followers? This question opens up several important aspects of Lucan spirituality.

First, he is experienced as present *through the Holy Spirit*. In Luke's first volume, apart from the first two chapters (where the Spirit comes upon John, Mary, Elizabeth, Zechariah and

Simeon), the Holy Spirit functions solely through Jesus (cf. 3.16, 22; 4.1, 14, 18; 10.21). In Luke's second volume, however, the presence of the Holy Spirit is all-pervasive, from the mighty events of Pentecost onwards. Now that Jesus reigns as Lord at God's right hand in heaven, his work is carried on by the apostles and the churches in the power and under the guidance of the Spirit whom Jesus sends (Luke 3.16; 24.49; Acts 1.1–2, 5, 8; 2.1ff., 17ff.; etc.). In Acts 16.6–7, moreover, the Holy Spirit is identified explicitly as 'the Spirit *of Jesus*', who guides the apostles in the direction which their mission should take. We are on firm ground, therefore, in claiming that, for Luke, Christian experience of God and of his Christ in the time of the church is in fundamental continuity with the disciples' experience of being with Jesus in the period of his earthly ministry. The same Spirit which inspired and empowered him, inspires and empowers them: so much so, that it is understood as the Spirit of Jesus himself.

A second way in which the continuing vitality and presence of the heavenly Lord is experienced is *through his name*. As MacRae points out, 'The application of Joel 2:32 to Jesus in the Pentecost discourse of Peter sets the tone for the whole book: "And it shall be that whoever calls on the name of the Lord shall be saved" (Acts 2:21).'[34] Thus, believers in Acts are known as those who call upon the Lord's name (9.14, 21; 22.16); salvation comes through calling upon the name (4.12); the forgiveness of sins is mediated through the name (10.43); baptism into the community of God's people and into the gift of the Spirit is baptism in the name of Jesus (2.38; 8.16; 10.48; 19.5); the apostles preach in the name (4.17–18; 9.27–9); they perform healings and exorcisms in the name (3.6; 16.18); and they suffer for the name (5.41; 9.16; cf. 26.9). Set against a biblical understanding of the reality and power of the name of God as God's immanent presence focused particularly upon Jerusalem and the temple (cf. 1 Kings 8.27–30), the constant invocation by the apostles of the name of the Lord now risen and ascended to God's right hand makes good sense. It is a way of expressing the apostles' awareness of the immanence of Christ while at the same time preserving the sense of his transcendence.

A third way in which the ascended Lord is present to his followers is *in the apostolic preaching of salvation history*. From being a figure purely of the past, Jesus becomes present to

93

responsive hearers in the testimony of the apostles.[35] That is one of the reasons why Luke gives such prominence, in his second volume, to the apostolic preaching. Note, for example, Peter's speech to Cornelius in Acts 10.34–43. The speech is so vibrant with Christ's resurrection power to save that, even before Peter has finished speaking (10.44a), 'the Holy Spirit fell on all who heard the word' (10.44b)! Similarly, Paul's sermon in the synagogue at Pisidian Antioch (13.16b–41). The recital of the story of Jesus is set within the larger story of salvation history from the exodus to King David and, as the fulfilment of Scripture, is presented as the culmination of God's mighty acts for the salvation of the family of Abraham and all who fear God. Concerning this story, Paul says: 'to us has been sent the message of this salvation (*ho logos tes sauterias tautes*)' (13.26b). So powerful and full of saving grace is this *logos*, that Luke tells us that, at the conclusion, 'many Jews and devout converts to Judaism followed Paul and Barnabas, who spoke to them and urged them to continue in the grace of God (*prosmenein tei chariti tou theou*)' (13.43). There can be no doubt that, according to Luke, the kerygmatic preaching about Jesus brings Jesus the Christ into the present as Saviour.

Finally, there is one further way in which the ascended Lord is present to his followers on earth: namely, *in the lives, and especially the sufferings, of his witnesses*. The fact that the stories of Jesus' followers in the Acts resemble quite closely the story of the life of Jesus in the gospel bears this out. In fact, this patterning is the literary device which Luke uses to make his point. The imitation of Christ in the lives of his followers—and they are not just the apostles—makes the exalted Christ present to the world.[36] Like the healing miracles of Jesus, the healing miracles of the apostles and missionaries bring salvation, in Jesus' name.[37] The same is true of the exorcisms, performed first by Jesus and subsequently by his emissaries.[38] The journey of Jesus to Jerusalem (Luke 9.51–19.44) preaching the good news of salvation likewise finds its imitation in the journey of Paul to Jerusalem (Acts 19.21–21.14). Importantly also, the sufferings of Jesus in the gospel find their imitation in the sufferings of his witnesses in the Acts (Acts 8.59–60, for Stephen; 9.15–16; 20.19–23, for Paul).[39] More precisely, we may say that it is by virtue of their imitation of Christ that his followers function as witnesses. Not only do they make Christ present to the world by preaching 'the message of his salvation'; they also make him present by embodying him in their lives.

It is to this theme of *witness* that I wish to turn next, in more detail. For, in the spirituality of Luke-Acts, 'witness' is one way of talking about the 'horizontal' corollary of the features of Lucan spirituality we have surveyed so far. To put it another way, the spirituality of Luke is certainly personal, but it is not privatized: it is a matter of concern to individuals, but it is not individualistic. So, in relation to what we have observed already, it is clear that the joy of which Luke speaks is a personal experience which at the same time is shared by many, both on earth and in heaven (cf. Luke 2.10–14; 15; Acts 2.46–7). The repentance and conversion upon which he places such stress are the means of personal salvation, certainly: but this salvation includes groups of persons, as well as individuals, and it leads to social reform and restitution, as well as a renewed spiritual discipline (cf. Luke 19.1–10; Acts 2.44–5). Faith, likewise, brings personal salvation, but it is associated at the same time also with healings of a quite public and social kind, a reorientation of the believer's outlook and behaviour, and entry into a fellowship: 'And all who believed were together and had all things in common' (Acts 2.44f.). Even prayer has a strong 'horizontal' and corporate dimension. The disciple who prays as Jesus taught will pray, 'Give us each day our daily bread; and forgive us our sins, for we ourselves forgive every one who is indebted to us' (Luke 11.3–4). He or she will remember the examples of Jesus and Stephen who die with a prayer on their lips for the forgiveness of their enemies. Prayer, also, is an activity which the church in Acts engages in together (e.g. Acts 1.14; 2.42; etc.). Finally, experience of the risen Lord, whether mediated through experiences of the Spirit, or baptism in 'the name', or hearing the apostolic kerygma, or the witness of the *imitatio Christi* in the lives of his followers, is something which is neither privatized nor individualistic. The Pentecostal experience results in preaching, repentance and community formation; Stephen's vision of the heavenly Son of Man enables him to testify to his persecutors at the cost of his life; and the christophany to Saul converts him to mission among his fellow Jews and the Gentiles.

That witness is a central concern of Lucan spirituality in its more 'horizontal' dimension cannot be doubted. First, Luke's two volumes themselves are intended as a witness to Theophilus of the truth about Jesus, as the prologues to each volume make clear (Luke 1.1–4; Acts 1.1ff.). We may say even that Luke's *writing* is an expression of his own spirituality of witness. Second, Luke's narrative is punctuated by long canticles, speeches, sermons, dialogues, and so on, usually in a public domain, all of which function as testimonies to the mighty acts of God in salvation and judgment and to the coming of the new age. Third, the miracle stories which fill both volumes have a strong evidential purpose.[40] The miracles of Jesus in the gospel demonstrate that 'the power of the Lord (*dunamis kuriou*) was with him to heal' (5.17b; Luke only; cf. Acts 2.22). The 'signs and wonders' (*semeia kai terata*) performed by the apostles and Paul in the Acts demonstrate likewise the outworking of the divine *dunamis* with the coming of the Spirit at Pentecost, though now it is the power of the Lord Jesus in heaven, mediated by the invocation of his name (cf. Acts 2.19, 43; 4.30; 5.12; 6.8; 8.6, 13; 14.3; 15.12).[41]

Fourth, Luke gives unparalleled attention to the theme of mission. As well as the sending out of the Twelve (9.1–6 par. Mark 6.6b–13), Luke alone narrates the sending on mission of the Seventy (-two) (10.1–20); and his second volume is a carefully constructed narrative of the programmatic missionary witness of the church, in fulfilment of the Lord's commission that, 'you shall be my witnesses in Jerusalem and in all Judea and Samaria and to the end of the earth' (Acts 1.8; cf. Luke 24.47–8). Fifth, the terminology of 'witness' is common, especially in the Acts. Here, *marturein* ('to bear witness') occurs eleven times, and *martus* ('one who bears witness') occurs thirteen times. The role of witness, furthermore, is how Luke characterizes the apostles. The qualifications listed by Peter for the replacement of Judas make this explicit: 'So one of the men who have accompanied us during all the time that the Lord Jesus went in and out among us . . . must become with us a witness (*martura*) to his resurrection' (Acts 1.22).

Finally, Luke habitually stresses the public nature of the events he narrates, in a way which gives them the character of open testimony.[42] The woman with the haemorrhage is a good instance from the gospel (8.47; diff. Mark 5:33): 'And when the woman saw *that she was not hidden*, she came trembling, and falling down before him *declared in the presence of all the people* why she had touched him, and how she had been immediately healed.' In a trial scene in the Acts, Paul says, in relation to King Agrippa, 'For *the king knows about these things*, and to him I speak freely; for I am persuaded that none of these things has escaped his notice, *for this was not done in a corner*' (Acts 26.26; cf. 2.22; 19.17). The same effect is created by the use of the terms *parresia* ('boldness') and *parresiazesthai* ('to speak boldly'). Noteworthy is Acts 4.13: 'Now when they saw the boldness (*ten parresian*) of Peter and John . . . they were amazed; and *they recognized that they had been with Jesus*'. Their boldness is itself a testimony to the power of Jesus and his word (cf. also, 4.29, 31). Even more striking is the fact that the Acts ends on this note, with Paul in Rome, 'preaching the kingdom of God and teaching about the Lord Jesus Christ quite openly and unhindered (*meta pases parresias akolutos*)' (28.31; cf. also 9.27f.; 13.46; 14.3; 18.26; 19.8; 26.26).

We have very good grounds, therefore, for interpreting Lucan spirituality as a *public spirituality* in which bold and open testimony to the grace of God is fundamental. Why should Luke place such importance on this aspect? There are a number of possibilities.

The first and most obvious is that Luke's public spirituality is an outworking of his sense of the unrestricted grace of God. The witness must bear the character of the One to whom witness is borne. If Jesus is 'a light (*phos*) for revelation to the Gentiles and for glory to thy people Israel' (2.32), then following Jesus involves bearing witness to that light before Jews and Gentiles (cf. 8.16; 11.33–6). Striking is the fact that the metaphor applied to Jesus in the Gospel is applied subsequently to the Christian missionaries in the Acts: '. . . For so the Lord has commanded us, saying, "I have set you to be a light for the Gentiles, that you may bring salvation to the uttermost parts of the earth"' (Acts 13.47; cf. also 26.17–18). If the gospel is good news for the poor, the captives, the blind, and the oppressed (Luke 4:18), then the appropriate response is to give alms to the poor, to set the captives free, to heal the blind, and to rescue the oppressed. This involves public action and bold testimony, precisely what Luke records of both Jesus and the early church. If Jesus is the Lord at God's right hand in heaven, then all creation is under him and public testimony must be borne before all. So, the Lord says of Saul, 'he is a chosen instrument of mine to carry my name before the Gentiles and kings and the sons of Israel' (Acts 9.15; cf. 22.15; 26.16–18).

Another reason for Luke's stress on the public dimension of Christian spirituality may be that he wishes to encourage his fellow believers that they have nothing to hide, that discipleship of the risen Lord requires missionary proclamation after the pattern of Jesus, the apostles and Paul, and that resistance and opposition to open testimony only leads to greater success.[43] In a word, there is something of the heroic in Lucan spirituality. The Spirit-inspired progress of the gospel *will triumph* in all the world. Thus, in the first volume, great emphasis is placed on the appeal of the good news to 'all the people' of Israel (cf. 1.10; 2.10; 3.15, 18, 21; 6.17; 7.1, 16, 29; 8.47; 9.13; 18.43; 19.47–8; etc.); responsibility for the rejection of Jesus is placed firmly with the corrupt leaders (cf. 19.47–8; 20.19, 20; 22.1–2, 52–3; 23.1–5; etc.; also, Acts 4.9–10; 13.27); and Jesus dies a serene martyr's death, only to be resurrected and exalted to heaven, from whence he will send the Spirit to enable his work of salvation to continue undiminished and even augmented. This is reinforced in volume two, where the mission to Jews and Gentiles progresses inexorably and with remarkable numerical success (cf. Acts 2.41, 47b; 4.4; 6.1a; etc.); where opposition serves only to give the movement notoriety and opportunities to defend itself publicly and in high places; where stories of amazing conversions—even of one of the movement's most violent opponents—are common; and where the final scene depicts that most famous convert preaching and teaching 'openly and unhindered' in Rome (28.30–1). Such a story is designed, in all likelihood, to strengthen the faint-hearted and to foster an ethos of hope and optimism grounded, theologically, in a belief in the inevitable and triumphant fulfilment of the divine plan.

The flip-side of the preceding is that Luke's stress on open witness has an element of political apologetic about it. Luke may be concerned to counter the suspicion that Christianity is a secretive and politically subversive religious sect from the East.[44] That helps to explain why Luke's version of the Passion so strongly emphasizes the innocence of Jesus. Pilate, the Roman governor, confirms it no fewer than three times (23.4, Luke only; 23.13–16, Luke only; 23.22b, Luke only); and the Roman centurion at the cross testifies, according to Luke alone, 'Certainly, this man was innocent (*dikaios*)!' (23.47; diff. Mark 15.39). In the Acts, such an apologetic motive helps to explain a number of things: the animus towards the leaders of the temple and synagogue communities as the real troublemakers (cf. Acts 4.1–2; 5.17–18; 6.8ff.; 8.1–3; etc.); the neutral role of the Roman officials trying to maintain the public order, even to the point of saving Christian missionaries from the lynch-mob (e.g. 21.27ff); the prominence given to the conversion of the centurion, Cornelius (10.1–11:18); the advantage to Paul of his Roman citizenship, exercised in his appeal to Caesar (25.8–12; cf. also, 16.37–8; 22.25ff.; 23.27); and the favourable reception given to Paul by figures of Roman authority, indicated, on the one hand, by the conversion of the proconsul Sergius Paulus (13.4–12) and, on the other, by the relative freedom granted to him in Rome itself (28.14b-31).

If Lucan spirituality has public testimony as one of its basic ingredients, we ought to consider, finally, the motif of the journey as providing the overall context in which this testimony takes place. For there can be little doubt that journeys and journeying provide, not only a fundamental literary device for ordering Luke's entire narrative, but also an important conceptual device for representing what Luke considers essential to the life of faith.[45] We will focus attention on the gospel, and in particular on its most distinctive literary feature, widely recognized to be a creative editorial construction, namely the travel narrative of 9.51–19.44.[46] We will see that both this narrative and others to which it points provide strong justification for depicting the spirituality of Luke as a *journey spirituality*.

The fact that the Lucan Jesus gives some of his most important teaching about discipleship in the setting of a travel narrative is noteworthy. On the one hand, the journey context gives Jesus' words and deeds revelatory significance, since in biblical and post-biblical terms, journeys are where God or a messenger of God makes himself and his will known to his people.[47] Elsewhere in Luke's narrative, we need think only of the revelation of the risen Lord to the two disciples on the road to Emmaus (Luke

24.13–35), the conversion of the Ethiopian eunuch on 'the road that goes down from Jerusalem to Gaza' (Acts 8.26–39), and the revelation of the risen Lord to Saul on the road to Damascus (9.1–9). On the other hand, the journey context fits, at the conceptual level, with the designation in the Acts of the Christian faith as 'the way (*he hodos*)' (at 9.2; 19.9, 23; 22.4; 24.14, 22) and of Jesus as the *archegos* ('pioneer', 'leader', at Acts 5.31; cf. Heb. 2.10; 12.2). It is appropriate, therefore, to interpret the Lucan teaching as intended to foster a strong sense of *the life of faith as a journey with the Lord Jesus in the context of which he makes known the qualities of character he requires of his followers*.

Turning to what *this* journey reveals about the qualities of character required for the life of faith, we note, first, that primary attention is given to the necessity of wholehearted commitment to the point of letting go external supports.[48] At the very beginning of the journey, Luke quite deliberately places a series of three sayings from the tradition about the necessity of radical detachment from worldly affairs and obligations for the sake of the kingdom of God (9.57–62). For the missionary, this will include home and family ties (9.57–62; cf. 10.1–12), but the same principle applies to every follower of the Christ.

In particular, the Lucan Jesus warns repeatedly about the danger of attachment to riches as an obstacle to discipleship, and calls for the positive use of wealth, especially in the form of giving alms to the poor.[49] In the sermon on the plain, there are the distinctive woes against the rich and prosperous, warning them of the sharp reversal in their fortunes which is to come (6.24–26). There is also the encouragement to 'lend, expecting nothing in return' (6.35b). These themes are taken further in the travel narrative: above all, in two substantial blocks of teaching. First, in 12.13–34, Luke brings together a collection of traditions around the theme of possessions. The parable of the rich fool (12.13–21, Luke only) is a sharp warning against the sin of covetousness.[50] This is followed by tradition which focuses on the problem of anxiety about possessions (12.22–32 par. Matt. 6.25–33) and the need for absolute trust in God's fatherly providence. The culmination of the teaching is striking. Where Matthew's version has, 'Do not lay up for yourselves treasure on earth' (Matt. 6:19ff.), Luke's has, 'Sell your possessions and give alms' (Luke 12.33f.). Luke is interested, not only in detachment from possessions, but in their redistribution as well. We are reminded immediately of the example of Zacchaeus, near the end of the travel narrative (19.1–10), who shows his repentance by his generous restitution and giving of alms ('the half of my goods', v. 8) to the poor.[51] The second block of teaching on the use and abuse of riches, is 16.1–31, which consists primarily of two parables unique to Luke, each of which begins, 'There was a rich man . . .'. The parable of the unjust steward (16.1–13) is addressed to disciples, and is a call to be wise in the use of wealth: by being generous in giving alms, the disciple lays up for him/herself a heavenly reward (especially vv. 9, 10–13). The parable of the rich man and Lazarus (16.19–31) is the converse of the preceding parable. It is addressed to 'the Pharisees', that is, to hypocrites, whose love of money hinders them from their duty under God's law to give to the poor (noting especially vv. 14–15, 16–17, 29). For such as these, only reversal and judgment lies in store.

Putting all this another way, what Jesus teaches about wealth and the obligation upon the rich to give to the poor expresses in a particular way the fundamental principle of *single-minded love of God and love of neighbour*. This is a second quality of character enunciated by Jesus on the journey. It comes in 10.25–28, in Jesus' dialogue with the lawyer. The two stories which follow immediately show, in chiastic fashion, what such love means. The good Samaritan (10.29–37, Luke only) shows what it means to love your neighbour. What the Samaritan does is a practical example of the teaching of Jesus himself in the sermon on the plain, where the love command is so central (6.27–36). Thus, the love shown by the Samaritan is love expressed in action; it is love for someone who has been made poor; it is love for an enemy; it involves personal and material sacrifice; it is open-ended; and it is non-reciprocal. The story of Mary and Martha (10.38–42, Luke only), on the other hand, shows what it means to love God. Such love is personified by Mary who is depicted, not distracted by worldly domestic cares like Martha, but serenely sitting in the position of a disciple, at the Lord's feet (cf. likewise, the Gerasene demoniac, at 8.35; also, Acts 22.3), listening to his word (*logos*). The effect of the juxtaposition of the two stories is striking. The story of Mary and

101

Martha 'is an important corrective to the impression which might otherwise be gained from the parable of the Samaritan. The two commandments of love are one, but neither component can be reduced to the other. Obedience, important as it is, can only follow from a hearing of the word of Jesus.'[52]

Obviously related to the right use of wealth and the double command of love is the massive encouragement of *an ethic of open, boundary-crossing hospitality.*[53] This is a third quality of Christian character to which attention is drawn on the journey, for it is the journey setting which makes hospitality such an apt concern. We may summarize Luke's understanding as follows. First, Christian hospitality is rooted in the practice of Jesus: 'Now the tax collectors and sinners were all drawing near to him. And the Pharisees and the scribes murmured, "This man receives sinners and eats with them"' (15.1–2; cf. 5.29–32; 7.34, 36–50). Second, as these verses indicate, such boundary-crossing hospitality generates hostility from the guardians of those boundaries (cf. 7.36–50). Third, hospitality is an active expression of the good news of God's solidarity with the poor. It is noticeable, in Luke's version of the parable of the great supper (14.15–24 par. Matt. 22.1–10), that the ones who refuse the invitation are people preoccupied with concerns of property and household, while the ones who are brought in are 'the poor and maimed and blind and lame'. Fourth, table-fellowship and table-talk are the starting mechanism of a new kind of society, marked out by humility (14.7–11) and non-reciprocal generosity. As Jesus says provocatively to his Pharisee host, 'When you give a dinner or a banquet, do not invite your friends or your brothers or your kinsmen or your rich neighbours, lest they also invite you in return, and you be repaid. But when you give a feast invite the poor, the maimed, the lame, the blind, and you will be blessed, because they cannot repay you' (14.12–14). Fifth, Christian hospitality is something shared between men and women and between Jew and Gentile. The former is illustrated in the story of Martha and Mary in 10.38–42 (cf. 7.36–50; 8.1–3). The latter is a major development in the book of Acts, from the Cornelius story on. Finally, such hospitality has an eschatological dimension to it. It is an anticipation of the messianic banquet in the kingdom of God (cf. 14.15; 22.14ff.; 24.28–35). That is why the element of joy is never far away. It is there in the series of three parables of the lost, set in the context of the reference to Jesus' subversive table-fellowship (15.1–32, at vv. 6–7, 9–10, 22–4, 32). It is there also, at the end of the journey, when Jesus goes as guest to the house of Zacchaeus, and Zacchaeus experiences the joyous salvation of the eschatological 'today' (19.1–10, at vv. 5b, 9).[54]

The mention of eschatology brings us to one other quality of character which the Jesus of Luke seeks to inculcate on the journey: namely, *readiness for the parousia*. While it is true that Luke plays down the doctrine of an *imminent* parousia,[55] it is nevertheless also the case that Luke's sense of an ending remains strong. The Son of Man will come suddenly, and it is imperative to be prepared. Teaching on this comes in 12.35–48, where two groups are addressed. Verses 35–40 use parables of a master returning from a wedding feast and the coming of a thief in the night to call everyone to a state of perpetual readiness, 'for the Son of man is coming at an unexpected hour' (12.40). Verses 41–8, which open with a question from Peter (v. 41, Luke only), are addressed more specifically to leaders—in the post-Easter situation, these would be Christian leaders in particular. They are warned, again in parables, against the abuse of their positions as leaders, teaching paralleled subsequently in Paul's address to the Ephesian elders, in Acts 20.28ff. Again, the motif of readiness in view of the sudden parousia is dominant: 'the master of that servant will come on a day when he does not expect him and at an hour he does not know . . .' (12.46).

Luke returns to this eschatological theme in a loose and difficult collection of traditions, in 17.20–18.8. Here, Jesus warns against attempts to say when the kingdom of God will come (17.20–1, Luke only); teaches that 'the day' of the Son of Man will be universal and will catch people unawares, preoccupied with the mundane concerns of 'marriage and giving in marriage' (17.22–37); and, in the parable of the unjust judge, referred to earlier, calls for an enduring faith in the coming of the Son of Man, nourished by persistent prayer (18.1–8).[56]

But while the parousia will be sudden, it will not be soon. Luke's introduction to the parable of the pounds (19.11–27, at v. 11, Luke only), located at the end of the journey, is indicative of this: 'He proceeded to tell a parable, because he was near to Jerusalem, *and because they supposed that the kingdom of God was to appear immediately'.* The parable addresses the question of how to be a disciple in the period between the resurrection/ ascension of Jesus (cf. v. 12) and his return. Like the teaching in 12.35–48, it is a summons to readiness and to accountability to the master in respect of the commission he has given.

This is reiterated, most significantly, in Jesus' final teaching discourse, in the temple, after he has arrived at Jerusalem. If we pay particular attention to the Lucan redaction of the apocalyptic discourse of Mark 13, in Luke 21.5–36, we note two things. First, the systematic attempt to counteract a doctrine of the imminence of the end, such that now, for example, the one who comes saying, 'The time is at hand (*ho kairos engiken*)', is a *false* messiah (21.8; diff. Mark 13.6, and cf. Mark 1.15)! Second, we note an important Lucan addition, which concerns how to be prepared in the longer period of time now envisaged before the end. This comes as the culmination of the discourse, in 21.34–6, and we are not surprised to find that attention focuses on: the danger of being weighed down by worldly cares; the need to 'watch at all times'; and the importance of prayer for the strength to endure in the hard times ahead. By comparison with Mark's more apocalyptic outlook, then, Luke's is *a spirituality of the long haul*, oriented on perseverance and faithful witness, 'until the times of the Gentiles are fulfilled' (21.24b; diff. Mark 13.20).

Conclusion

I have tried to describe and explain a number of the main features of the spirituality of Luke-Acts, understanding that spirituality as Luke's vision of the Christian way lived in response to the grace of God revealed in Jesus and imparted by the Spirit. By way of a brief conclusion, I wish to offer some comments on aspects of the Lucan vision which appear to me inadequate or (what is much more likely) which I do not properly understand.

There is, first, the issue of *the unabashed supernaturalism* of Luke's narrative. I have in mind here, for instance, the fact that Luke embroiders the story of the call of Simon (and his partners) with the story of the miraculous catch of fish (5.1–11; diff. Mark 1.16–20; cf. also, John 21.1–14), so that Simon's response of penitence is a response to a marvel: 'For he was astonished, and all that were with him, at the catch of fish which they had taken (v. 9). In other words, Simon and his colleagues become followers because of the miracle they have witnessed. Similarly, whereas Mark prefaces the sending of the twelve on mission with the ominous episode of Jesus' rejection in Nazareth (Mark 6.1–6a), Luke prefaces it with four miracle stories (8.22–56), implying that the mission of the disciples will be effective likewise; and such it proves to be (9.6). Yet again, whereas Mark tends to subordinate the miracles of Jesus to his teaching, Luke gives miracles and teaching equal weight (cf. 4.31–37 diff. Mark 1.21–8; cf. also 5.12–15 diff. Mark 4.40–5). Clearly, for Luke, miracles validate Jesus by showing who he is.[57] In Luke's version of John's question about Jesus (7.18–23 par. Matt. 11.2–6), therefore, we find that John's inquiry comes after he hears of two miracles performed by Jesus—the healing of the centurion's servant (7.1–10) and the raising of the widow's son at Nain (7.11–17) —and also that the inquiry is met with the response that, 'In that hour he cured many of diseases and plagues and evil spirits, and on many that were blind he bestowed sight' (7.21, Luke only).

The picture of the miraculous in Acts is consistent with this. Miracles have a definite evidential value and certainly provide a basis for faith. Thus, Peter heals the paralytic Aeneas (as Jesus has healed a paralytic, according to Luke 5.17–26), with the result that 'immediately he rose. And all the residents of Lydda and Sharon saw him, *and they turned to the Lord*' (Acts 9.32–35, at vv. 34b–35). Again, Peter raises Tabitha from the dead (as Jesus has raised Jairus' daughter and the son of the widow of Nain), with the result that 'it became known throughout all Joppa, *and many believed in the Lord*' (Acts 9.36–43, at v. 42). Such examples could be multiplied. Overall, the apostles are workers of 'signs and wonders' (e.g. 2.43; 5.12; 6.8; 8.6; 14.3; 15.12), and these miraculous deeds provide the foundation for a response of belief, in a context of missionary expansion.

One wonders if we do not have here a recipe for a faith which is superficial at best, an open invitation to a 'seeing-is-believing' kind of spirituality. Gone is the reticence of a Paul to speak about manifestations of the supernatural. He 'boasts', instead, of his suffering (cf. 2 Cor. 10–13). Gone is the determination of a Mark to subordinate miracles to teaching and to the narrative of the Passion. Gone is the tendency of a Mark or a Matthew to turn a miracle story into an allegory of discipleship. Likewise, the deep christological symbolism of the Johannine 'signs' is missing. This is to put the difference between Luke-Acts and these other writings too starkly, to be sure: but it helps, perhaps, to make the point. The rather unsubtle supernaturalism of Luke's narrative has too much of the whiff of propaganda about it to make it a satisfactory summons to a spirituality which is more than skin-deep.

Linked with this is *the tendency towards triumphalism* in Luke's vision of things.[58] This manifests itself in a number of ways. In the portrait of Jesus' passion, for instance, the strong element of lone struggle and bitter agony in Mark is transformed into a portrait which is remarkably eirenic. In Luke, the focus is on the truly good and righteous man whose compassion and trust in God overcome evil. At his arrest, he performs one last miracle of healing, to restore the right ear of the high priest's slave (22.50–1, Luke only). On the way to the cross, he speaks words of compassion for the women of Jerusalem (23.28–31, Luke only). On the cross, he speaks words of forgiveness towards his enemies and of trust in God to whom he commits himself (23.34, 43, 46). Then, his righteousness is rewarded by resurrection, ascension, and exaltation to God's right hand.

In the portrait of the apostles and of the apostolic church, there is a similar tendency. There is no mention of the disciples fleeing in terror from the garden. The story of Simon Peter's denial has its teeth drawn when Jesus assures Simon at the last supper of his prayers for his deliverance from Satan (22.31–2, Luke only). They are there at the cross, we may assume (23.49 diff. Mark 15:40–1). They receive appearances of the risen Lord who instructs them over a forty day period (24.13–49; Acts 1.3ff.). They are witnesses of the ascension (Acts 1.9ff.). And they then embark on a mission of extraordinary success, from Jerusalem as far as Rome itself, a mission empowered by the Spirit, accompanied by angelophanies, authenticated by 'signs and wonders', overcoming opposition, and generating a following running into thousands. There is no evidence of doubts surrounding the apostolic credentials of Paul (cf. 1 Cor. 9.1–2), nor of serious tension between Paul and Peter at Antioch (cf. Gal. 2.11ff.), nor of sharp conflict over the acceptance of a law-free mission to Gentiles (cf. Gal. 1–2). Instead, on the latter point, the sweet reasonableness of a church council prevails, and a compromise is reached (Acts 15.1–29). The eirenic spirit of Jesus is replicated in the eirenic spirit of the church. The overall accent is one of steady progress in a context of miraculous guidance and in fulfilment of a divine plan for the salvation of the world.

Such a narrative generates a sense of assurance, even optimism, to be sure; and that can be helpful as an antidote to despair when the going gets rough, as in times of persecution, for instance. But whether it is the best antidote to despair is another matter. It is a fine line between a triumphal account of times past as a basis for perseverance in the present and hope for the future, and, on the other hand, a triumphal account of times past which becomes a temptation to a false consciousness unable to respond in a realistic manner to the contingencies of daily discipleship in a hostile world. Luke does not lead inevitably in either direction, but it is as well to be aware of the possibilities. Perhaps the final vignette of Luke's two volumes maintains a helpful balance. Yes: Paul preaches the kingdom and teaches about Christ, 'openly and unhindered' (28.31). But no: he does so under armed guard (28.16), his preaching is rejected by the leaders among his Jewish compatriots (28.17–28), and his final fate is left undetermined. If there is triumphalism—and I think there is—then it is certainly not as strident as it could be. To put it another way, the tension between the 'now' and the 'not yet', in Luke's story of salvation history, remains. The 'kingdom of God' which Paul preaches from his captivity in Rome is, for Luke, definitely still to come.

Notes

1. On the unity of Luke-Acts and the overall purpose of the work, see the recent survey by I.H. Marshall, 'Luke and his "Gospel"', in P. Stuhlmacher, ed., *Das Evangelium und die Evangelien* (Tübingen: Mohr/Siebeck, 1983), pp. 289–307.
2. So, too, R.E. Brown, *The Churches the Apostles Left Behind* (New York: Paulist Press, 1984), pp. 65–8.
3. Cf. Luke 1.15, 35, 41, 67; 2.25, 26, 27; Acts 1.2, 5, 8, 16; 2.4, 17, 18, 33; etc..
4. Luke seems to have a particular interest in angels. In Luke 1–2,

there are fourteen references to an *angelos*; and in Acts as a whole, twenty-one references. See the useful discussion of H.J. Richards, in *The First Christmas: What Really Happened?* (London: Mowbray, 1973), ch. 6.

5. W. Morrice, *Joy in the New Testament* (Grand Rapids: Eerdmans, 1985), p. 91. I am indebted to the book as a whole for what follows in this section.

6. In 6.23, persecuted believers are told by Jesus to 'Rejoice (*charete*) in that day, and leap for joy (*skirtesate*), for behold, your reward is great in heaven'. So even in adversity, as well as at times of great favour, joyous exultation is an appropriate response.

7. Cf. also B.E. Beck, *Christian Character in the Gospel of Luke* (London: Epworth Press, 1989), pp. 61–5, noting especially the statement at p. 62: 'Through thanksgiving joy is focussed in a discernment of God as the giver; but . . . it is a recognition, not primarily of what God is but of what he has done. In the coming of Jesus the awaited new age has dawned and people enjoy its benefits (cf. 1.78; 2.20; 7.16). . . . It is 'eschatological joy', the rejoicing of the end-time when the kingdom has come.'

8. Beck, *Character*, p. 11.

9. Beck, *Character*, p. 11.

10. Cf. also, J.A. Fitzmyer, *Luke the Theologian: Aspects of his Teaching* (London: Chapman, 1989), p. 131.

11. See further, C.H. Talbert, *Reading Luke* (London: SPCK, 1990), pp. 84–9.

12. On which, see now, D.A. Neale, *None but the Sinners: Religious Categories in the Gospel of Luke* (Sheffield: JSOT, 1991).

13. I have discussed this further in my essay, 'Women, Jesus and the Gospels', in R. Holloway, ed., *Who Needs Feminism? Men Respond to Sexism in the Church* (London: SPCK, 1991), esp. pp. 43–8. See also the excellent, comprehensive essay by Mary D'Angelo, 'Women in Luke-Acts', *Journal of Biblical Literature*, 109 (1990), pp. 441–61.

14. See further, Talbert, *Luke*, pp. 149–52.

15. Beck, *Character*, pp. 127–44.

16. So, too, Talbert, *Luke*, pp. 175–7.

17. See further, Fitzmyer, *Luke the Theologian*, pp. 203–33; and F.J. Matera, *Passion Narratives and Gospel Theologies* (New York: Paulist Press, 1986), pp. 183–6.

18. Cf. Beck, *Character*, pp. 130–1: Luke 'also intends the Pharisees in his gospel to represent an internal threat because they exemplify a style of religion and life by which he believes Christians are in danger of being influenced. . . . Luke has fashioned the Pharisees, who already had a negative image in Christian tradition, so that

they embody those faults to which he believes the Christian readers are prone.' I am indebted to pp. 130–44 for the material which follows on 'the Pharisaic mind'.

19. Beck, *Character*, p. 138.
20. Other examples from the Acts include the conversion of the Samaritans (8.4ff.), Simon the magician (8.9–13), the Ethiopian eunuch (8.26–40), the Roman proconsul Sergius Paulus (13.4–12), Lydia of Thyatira (16.14–15), the Philippian jailer (16.25–34). Such stories express the breaking down of barriers between people of different nationalities, social status, gender, and so on, which the preaching of the gospel makes possible. Cf. Luke 24.47; Acts 1.8; and G. Krodel, *Acts* (Philadelphia: Fortress, 1981), p. 37ff..
21. For what follows, see Beck, *Character*, pp. 71–92; also, Fitzmyer, *Luke the Theologian*, pp. 130–1.
22. Beck, *Character*, p. 71.
23. Contrast Mark 5.36b, with the present continuous imperative, *pisteue*, and lacking the final clause altogether.
24. Beck, *Character*, p. 72.
25. Cf. Beck, *Character*, pp. 83–5, noting at p. 85: 'The interpretation of the parable of the sower is thus an important contribution negatively and positively to our picture of Christian faith after conversion and strongly emphasizes the idea of persistence.'
26. See further, A.A. Trites, 'The Prayer Motif in Luke-Acts', in C.H. Talbert, ed., *Perspectives on Luke-Acts* (Edinburgh: T&T Clark, 1978), pp. 168–86; also, Beck, *Character*, pp. 67–70; Fitzmyer, *Luke the Theologian*, pp. 136–7.
27. See further, J.A. Fitzmyer, 'The Composition of Luke, Chapter 9', in Talbert, ed., *Perspectives*, pp. 139–52.
28. See the excellent essay of B.E. Beck, 'Gethsemane in the Four Gospels', *Epworth Review*, 15 (1988), pp. 57–65, esp. pp. 60–3; also, Matera, *Passion Narratives*, pp. 166–9. With most commentators, I take 22.43–4 (telling of the angelophany and Jesus' bloody agony) to be early but secondary. See B.M. Metzger, *A Textual Commentary on the Greek New Testament* (London: United Bible Societies, 1975), p. 177; also, B.D. Ehrman and M.A. Plunkett, 'The Angel and the Agony: The Textual Problem of Luke 22:43–44', *Catholic Biblical Quarterly*, 45 (1983), pp. 401–16.
29. Cf. Acts 7.60, where Stephen, even while he is being stoned to death, kneels down to pray; also, 9.40 (Peter); 20.36 (Paul); 21.5b (Paul and his fellow-travellers, together with all the believers from Tyre).
30. See further, W. Moberly, 'Proclaiming Christ Crucified: Some Reflections on the Use and Abuse of the Gospels', *Anvil*, 5 (1988), pp. 31–52, at pp. 36–9.
31. A.A. Trites, 'Prayer Motif', p. 184.

32. See further, J.A. Fitzmyer, 'The Ascension of Christ and Pentecost', *Theological Studies*, 45 (1984), pp. 409–40.
33. Especially helpful is G.W. MacRae, '"Whom Heaven Must Receive Until The Time"': Reflections on the Christology of Acts', *Interpretation*, 27 (1973), pp. 151–65.
34. MacRae, 'Christology', p. 161.
35. Cf. the comment of Krodel, *Acts*, p. 5: 'The church lives not after Christ, but under him, and the Book of Acts deals with what Jesus continues to do and teach through his church in the power of the Spirit.'
36. Cf. the thought-provoking essay of C.H. Talbert, 'The Way of the Lukan Jesus: Dimensions of Lukan Spirituality', *Perspectives in Religious Studies*, 9 (1982), pp. 237–49, which suggests that 'Luke gives us a developmental picture of Jesus in which his individual progress in spirituality is depicted as the gradual unfolding of the divine plan in Jesus' way . . . [and that] Jesus' way is normative for his followers. As a pioneer, the Lukan Jesus has opened a way for life to be lived from the cradle to the grave and beyond' (pp. 246, 247). I have three difficulties with this. 1. Is it the case, given the presence of the Spirit with him from the beginning, that the Lucan Jesus shows signs of *development* in his understanding of God and the way he must go? 2. Is Talbert in danger of reading psychological theories of personal development and life-cycle stages into the story of Jesus as told by Luke? 3. Does Talbert's view of Jesus' way as normative for his followers leave any room for the distinctiveness of Jesus?
37. See further, P.J. Achtemeier, 'The Lukan Perspective on the Miracles of Jesus: A Preliminary Sketch', in Talbert, ed., *Perspectives*, pp. 153–67; also, G.W.H. Lampe, 'Miracles in the Acts of the Apostles', in C.F.D. Moule, ed., *Miracles* (London: Mowbray, 1965), pp. 165–78.
38. Cf., for both healings and exorcisms, the summary statements at Luke 4.40–41; 6.17–19; and Acts 5.12–16; 8.4–8. See further, G.H. Twelftree, *Christ Triumphant. Exorcism Then and Now* (London: Hodder & Stoughton, 1985), pp. 95–116.
39. See further, B.E. Beck, '"Imitatio Christi" and the Lucan Passion Narrative', in W. Horbury and B. McNeil, eds., *Suffering and Martyrdom in the New Testament* (Cambridge: Cambridge University Press, 1981), pp. 28–47.
40. On the way in which Luke skilfully balances material about teaching/preaching the word and stories of miraculous healings and exorcisms (as at Luke 4.18–22, 23–7) in such a way as to give them equal weight, see Achtemeier, 'Lukan Perspective', p. 156f..
41. Note Lampe's comment, in his essay, 'Miracles in the Acts', p. 171: 'Miracles are, therefore, in Luke's understanding of the

matter, part and parcel of the entire mission of witness. The whole
is miraculous, in so far as it is a continuous mighty work of God.'
42. So too, Beck, *Character*, p. 81ff..
43. See further, R.J. Karris, 'Missionary Communities: A New
Paradigm for the Study of Luke-Acts', *Catholic Biblical Quarterly*,
41 (1979), pp. 80–97.
44. I have discussed this in two essays, 'The *Acts of the Apostles* as
Evidence of the Relations between the Early Christian Communities and Roman Authority', and 'Roman Attitudes to Christianity
and the Correspondence of Pliny', in *Ancient Society: Resources
for Teachers*, 6 (Macquarie University, 1976), pp. 120–41, 142–50.
45. So too, P.J. Bernadicou, 'The Spirituality of Luke's Travel Narrative', *Review for Religious*, 36 (1977), pp. 455–66; also, C.H.
Talbert, 'Discipleship in Luke-Acts', in F.F. Segovia, ed., *Discipleship in the New Testament* (Philadelphia: Fortress, 1985), pp. 62–75.
46. See further, Talbert, *Luke*, pp. 111–82.
47. Cf. Gen. 16.1–16; 18.1–16; 19; Exodus, *passim*; Tobit 5–12; Mark
6.45–52; Heb. 13.2; also, Homer's *Odyssey*, XVII. 485–7.
48. So too, Beck, *Character*, p. 52.
49. Amongst the mountain of literature on this, see especially Beck,
Character, pp. 28–54; R.J. Karris, 'Poor and Rich: The Lukan *Sitz
im Leben*', in Talbert, ed., *Perspectives*, pp. 112–25, and the
literature cited there; also, L.T. Johnson, *Sharing Possessions*
(London: SCM Press, 1986). Karris, among others, argues that
Luke focuses so heavily on the dangers of riches and the importance of almsgiving and detachment from wealth because he is
addressing predominantly prosperous, Gentile converts who, lacking the biblical ethic of giving to the poor, need particular
encouragement and instruction in this direction, in order to prevent a damaging split between rich and poor in the church. He
says: 'Luke's *Sitz im Leben* consists of propertied Christians who
have been converted and cannot easily extricate themselves from
their cultural mindsets. It also consists of Christians in need of
alms. Luke takes great pains to show that Christians treat each
other as friends and that almsgiving and care for one another is of
the essence of the Way. If the converts do not learn this lesson and
learn it well, there is danger that the Christian movement may
splinter' ('Poor and Rich', p. 117).
50. Its parallel in the Acts narrative is the judgment story of Ananias
and Sapphira, in Acts 5.1–11.
51. The parallel in the Acts are the cameo portraits of the early
Christian fellowships, where 'all who believed were together and
had all things in common; and they sold their possessions and
goods and distributed them to all, as any had need' (Acts 2.44–5;
cf. 4.32–7; 6.1ff.; 11.27–30).
52. Beck, *Character*, p. 24.

111

53. See further, J. Koenig, *New Testament Hospitality* (Philadelphia: Fortress, 1985), pp. 85–123; R.J. Karris, 'Luke's Soteriology of With-ness', *Currents in Theology and Mission*, 12 (1985), pp. 346–52; H. Moxnes, 'Meals and the New Community in Luke', *Svensk Exegetisk Arsbok*, 51–2 (1986–87), pp. 158–67; and P.F. Esler, *Community and Gospel in Luke-Acts* (Cambridge: Cambridge University Press, 1987), pp. 71–109.

54. On *semeron* as highlighting the present reality of salvation in Lucan eschatology (cf. also, 2.11; 4.21; 5.26; 23.43), see Fitzmyer, *Luke the Theologian*, p. 129; and, in general, H. Conzelmann, *The Theology of Salvation* (London, 1960), pp. 95–136.

55. See further, C.K. Barrett, *Luke the Historian in Recent Study* (Philadelphia: Fortress, 1970), pp. 42f., 48f., and especially pp. 64ff..

56. Note Talbert's comment on 18.1–8, in *Luke*, p. 169: 'Here we confront the problem of doubt about whether the parousia will ever take place and the behaviour such doubt induces . . . As it stands in its context, the story functions as an encouragement to Christians not to give up hope for the parousia but to go on praying "Thy Kingdom come."'

57. See further, Achtemeier, 'Lukan Perspective', *passim*.

58. So too, Brown, *The Churches the Apostles Left Behind*, p. 69ff..

4
'You will know the truth and the truth will make you free'

THE SPIRITUALITY OF THE FOURTH GOSPEL

Introduction

Christian spirituality, as we have seen, is about the sense of the presence of God and living in the light of that presence. It is about living in response to the God who is revealed in Christ and who graces us with his Spirit. The Fourth Gospel is a natural place to go to reflect in a fundamental way on the nature of Christian spirituality. There are several reasons for this.

First, its place in the canon of scripture, as the fourth and last of the four gospels, means that it has a special significance. In its own way—whether or not this was the intention of its author, and I doubt that it was—it sums up and gives an authoritative interpretation to the message of the three synoptic gospels which have come before. It makes crystal clear what they have said differently and sometimes more obliquely or hesitantly about Jesus: namely, that he is God incarnate, the one who uniquely reveals God and the way to God. This authoritative presentation of God-in-Christ then provides the basis for what follows in scripture: the coming into being of the church and the mission of the church in anticipation of the consummation of history by God. So John's gospel has a pivotal role. It recapitulates and brings to a magisterial climax the message of the revelation of God in Christ and it paves the way for the life of the church founded on Christ. In terms of the canon, therefore, it seems legitimate to approach this gospel with high expectations of its relevance for spirituality.

Second, we also turn naturally to the Fourth Gospel because, from a very early point in its history, the church has acknowledged John as 'the spiritual gospel'. This is how it was described by Clement of Alexandria, in the second century; and there can be little doubt that he struck a chord which resonates truly for

113

many other readers of this gospel as well.[1] How else can we do justice to the profound revelatory utterances of the Jesus of John about, for example, the nature of true worship, or how to attain eternal life, or how to overcome the world? Down the centuries, the church has borne witness consistently to the continuing relevance of John for instruction and inspiration in the life of faith; so it is right and proper for us to acknowledge that tradition and test it out for ourselves.

Third, there is something about the content of the Fourth Gospel which renders it transparent for reflection on Christian spirituality. Fundamentally, there is the revelation of the divine glory, a call to believe, a way to go which leads to God, the offer of deliverance from darkness into light and from death to life, and a basis for assurance. In other words, John's gospel provides clear and authoritative answers to questions about God, the world, life and death, truth and goodness, and salvation and judgment. That is to put the matter in rather abstract terms; but it is just such terms and symbols which are all-pervasive in the gospel itself and which seem to give it the capacity to be relevant always and in a way which transcends time and space. When John says, '. . . these things are written that you may believe that Jesus is the Christ, the Son of God, and that believing you may have life in his name' (20.31), the addressee could be Everyman and Everywoman. Even though the gospel tells a story about the past in all its particularity, the way it is told gives it a credal quality, a symbolic depth and an existential appeal which allow it to reverberate into the present of every reader. It is not really surprising that it acknowledges no specific author and that the identity of its addressees can only be guessed at. Such characteristics allow John's gospel to take on a life of its own, almost independent of its historical origins.[2]

Johannine spirituality described

1. The first thing to say about the spirituality of the Fourth Gospel is that it is *a personal spirituality*. It has to do with persons in their relationships with God and one another. The main purpose of the gospel is to pass on the revelation which makes true relationship with God and one another possible. This revelation comes from God and comes in personal form: 'And

the Word became flesh and dwelt among us, full of grace and truth . . . No one has ever seen God; the only Son who is in the bosom of the Father, he has made him known' (1.14, 18). Because the revelation comes from God, it is an expression of divine grace: so that the life of faith is a life lived in response to that grace. And because the revelation comes in personal, incarnated form, it requires a personal, incarnated response.

This emphasis on the personal in Johannine spirituality is seen in a number of ways. First, the relationship between Jesus and God is presented in intensely personal terms. God is the Father and Jesus is the Son [3] As the Son, he comes from the Father, abides constantly in the Father, seeks always to do the work of the Father, shares in the glory of the Father, reveals himself as the way to the Father, and finally returns to the Father. This relationship between the Father and the Son is unique in its intensity of love, reciprocity and responsiveness: it uniquely expresses the 'eternal life' which Jesus offers to the world. Indeed, it is because the relationship is unique in this way that Jesus the Son is able to bring others into the relationship as children of the Father (1.12) and heirs of eternal life (3.16).

Second, the revelation of the love of the Father for the Son and for the world is made in the context of the life and death of a person in history. That is why the evangelist writes a gospel: a narrative of the life of Christ, someone who can be 'deeply moved' at the sorrow of others and who can weep himself (11.33–5), and who shows great love for his friends and is loved (and betrayed) in return. That is why, too, the evangelist tells of Galilee and Judea and Samaria, of John and the disciples, of Pharisees and the Jews, of the entry into Jerusalem, of Caiaphas and Pilate, and of a crucifixion by the Romans. The personal nature of Johannine spirituality is not purely private, individual and spiritual: it is embodied in the actions of persons in history.

Third, the revelation is conveyed in a narrative which is constructed around striking person-to-person encounters.[4] In these encounters, individuals bear personal witness. The Father bears witness to the Son (12.28), and the Son to the Father (1.18). John bears witness to Jesus (1.29, etc.); and so do many other people—Andrew, Philip, Nathaniel, and so on: the list would include every other character in the story! But particularly noticeable is the prominence this evangelist gives to very personal and intimate, one-to-one encounters: Jesus and Nicodemus (ch.3), Jesus and the Samaritan woman (ch.4), Jesus and the lame man (ch.5), Jesus and the blind man (ch.9), Jesus and 'his own' (chs.13–17), Jesus and Pilate (18.28–19.16), to list the most significant. Such encounters convey very strongly the sense that believing in Jesus is an inescapably personal matter requiring individual decision for or against him.[5]

It is this feature of Johannine spirituality which gives it such a powerful existential appeal. And rightly so. We sense in John something which is quite explicit in the life and writings of Søren Kierkegaard, one of the founders of modern existentialism—namely, an overwhelming acknowledgment of individual responsibility before God in the life of faith, and a certain hostility to the crowd and the religion of the crowd as poor arbiters of where truth lies.[6]

2. But if the spirituality of the Fourth Gospel is personal and involves an appeal to the individual, that is not to say that it is individualistic. On the contrary, there is a strong *sense of the corporate* in Johannine spirituality. This is a second important aspect of Johannine spirituality to which attention needs to be drawn, especially because the widespread tendency to interpret this gospel in individualistic terms does not do justice to the strong interpersonal dimension of the gospel's spiritual vision.[7]

First, the gospel proclaims God's love for 'the world' (*ho kosmos*) (3.16). Such a revelation transcends, displaces even, group boundaries of one kind—boundaries which the Pharisees, the Jews, Caiaphas and Pilate, amongst others, attempt to maintain. But in so doing, it proclaims as a reality a society of another kind. Members of this society are called 'children of God' (*tekna tou theou*), and include Jews, Samaritans and Greeks—for differences of race no longer symbolize differences of spiritual status, since believers are ones 'born, not of blood nor of the will of the flesh nor of the will of man, but of God' (1.13). Gender differences no longer symbolize differences of spiritual status, either: hence the prominence in this gospel of the mother of Jesus, the Samaritan woman, Martha and Mary with Lazarus, and Mary Magdalene.[8] The direct, personal, unmediated access to the Father which the divine Son makes possible, brings into being a new, reconstituted people of God.

The metaphors used to identify believers have a strong corporate dimension, as well. From the prologue comes the metaphor, 'children of God', already mentioned (1.12; cf. also 11.52; 1 John 3.1, 2, 10; 5.2).[9] From chapter 10 comes the image of the 'good shepherd' who 'lays down his life for the sheep' (vv. 11, 15), and who has 'other sheep that are not of this fold' whom the shepherd will bring also, with the result that 'there will be one flock, one shepherd' (v. 16). From chapter 15 comes the metaphor of the vine and the branches which focuses primarily on the relationship of branches to vine, but speaks at the same time of bearing a fruit which is identified as love. These metaphors of sheep and vine are corporate metaphors taken from scripture. There, they represent the nation of Israel. Now, provocatively, they are being used of God's new people, membership of which is restricted no longer to the descendants of Abraham (cf. 8.31–59). And, of course, in addition to these metaphors, the story itself presents significant groups of believers for us to identify with: the disciples; the family group of Martha, Mary and Lazarus, with whom Jesus has such a close bond; the Greeks, of 12.20ff. (cf.7.35); and the mother of Jesus and the beloved disciple at the foot of the cross (19.25–7).

The sense of corporateness in these metaphors and group portraits is reinforced by an ethic which emphasizes the centrality of the love commandment and the ideal of unity.[10] Whereas in the synoptic tradition, the command of Jesus is to love your enemies, it is striking that in the Johannine tradition, the commandment of Jesus (to the disciples) is to love *one another*. Furthermore, the great 'high priestly' prayer of Jesus to the Father at the last supper for the unity of his followers (ch.17) is unprecedented in the synoptics.

Most fundamental for an awareness of the corporate dimension in Johannine spirituality, however, is the exploration and exposition of the relationship of the Son and the Father, so distinctive of this gospel. For the present purpose, it is sufficient to note: first, that the relationship is one of mutual indwelling (14.10–11); second, that it is a relationship of love (14.31; 15.9; 17.23ff.); third, that it is one of identity of wills (15.10); and fourth, that it finds expression in the willing subordination of the

117

Son to the Father (14.28), so that Jesus functions as the divine agent sent from above to reveal God's glory in the world (17.1ff.). Some aspects of this relationship are unique: only Jesus is *the* Son in John, only Jesus is *the* way, and only Jesus goes ahead via the cross to prepare a place for those whom the Father has given him. On the other hand, it is clear also that the relationship of the Father and the Son provides the pattern for the relationship of mutual indwelling and subordination in love between Father, Son and believer. So, for example, John 15.9–10: 'As the Father has loved me, so have I loved you; abide in my love. If you keep my commandments, you will abide in my love, just as I have kept my Father's commandments and abide in his love.'

3. This leads naturally to a third major aspect of Johannine spirituality: it is *thoroughly christocentric*. This can hardly be overemphasized. The heart of the gospel concerns the revelation of God in Christ: Jesus as God incarnate. This means that, at the personal level, the life of faith starts and ends with believing in Jesus as the one—the only one—through whom God gives eternal life (3.16). At the corporate level, it means obeying the commandments of Jesus and acknowledging him alone as the good shepherd, the fulfilment of the messianic hopes of Israel and the people's true and only king (cf. 19.14–15). We become aware of John's christocentric focus for the life of faith if we consider what Jesus says and what Jesus does.

Starting with *what Jesus says*, it is noticeable that, whereas the Jesus of the synoptics comes proclaiming the 'kingdom of God' and calling people to acknowledge the divine sovereignty in their lives, the Jesus of John comes bearing witness to himself as the unique revelation of God and the way to God. Most characteristic of this emphasis are the great 'I AM' sayings,[11] the epitome of which is John 14.6: 'I am the way , the truth, and the life; no one comes to the Father but by me.' Significantly, there are seven of these symbolic 'I AM' sayings,[12] just as there are seven miracle-signs. Together, the sayings and the signs are mutually reinforcing in pointing to Jesus as the true and only source of life.

The implications of the 'I AM' sayings for Johannine spirituality are critical. First, because Jesus speaks as revealer, the sayings imply that the life of faith is a response to revelation, a response to grace — and that corresponds with both what we have found in the other gospels and with the pattern of biblical spirituality as a whole. Second, the sayings make the life of faith a response to Jesus as divine: for, in several instances, Jesus speaks the I AM in an absolute form (8.24, 28, 58; 13.19) reminiscent of the self-revelation of God in the Old Testament (e.g. Exod. 3.14, *LXX*). Third, the sayings make the life of faith a response to Jesus exclusively, and to none other. Now, Jesus is the life-giving bread, not Moses and the Torah (John 6; cf. Sirach 15.3; 24.19–21). Now, Jesus is the light, a symbol applied previously to Torah (e.g. in Ps. 119.105). Now, Jesus is the door and the way; and, once again, 'the way' is a symbol applied previously to Torah (e.g. Deut. 5.32–3). Now, Jesus is the shepherd, a symbol used of God and the leaders of the nation, in the Old Testament (e.g. Ps. 23; 78.70–2; 80; Isa. 40.11; Jer. 31.10; Ezek. 34; 37.24), and of the Teacher of Righteousness at Qumran. And, importantly, Jesus is the *good* shepherd who, in contrast to the leaders of Israel who are false shepherds (cf. Ezek. 34), lays down his life for the sheep (10.11ff.). All of this implies, fourth, that the life of faith in Johannine terms demands a personal choice: to 'receive' or 'believe in' the Jesus who makes these exclusive claims, or not. This either/or dimension brackets the entire gospel (cf. 1.17; 20.30–1) as well as punctuating it throughout.

What Jesus does according to the Fourth Gospel also draws attention to the christological focus of Johannine spirituality. First and foremost, Jesus is the one who comes from above (cf. 1.9; 3.19; 9.39; 11.27; 12.46; 16.28; 18.37). This is the burden of the first of the two main literary sections of the gospel (i.e. chs.1–12). He comes as the one sent by God to reveal the way to eternal life. As the one who comes, he brings salvation and judgment, and provokes decision. That is why conflict and controversy surround him. With the coming of the Son of God, things can never be the same again: neither the temple, nor the Torah, nor the festivals, nor the identities of Jews, Samaritans and Greeks, nor life as the people of God, nor even life and death itself.

In the second half of the story (chs.13–21), Jesus is the one who departs. This is important too. He departs by laying down

Re-creation

his life in death, and showing thereby that the life of faith is an escape neither from death nor from the consequences of faithful witness to the truth before the powers-that-be. In departing, he returns to the Father through death and resurrection to glorify the Father, to show that the world has been overcome, to prepare a place for those who come after, and to make possible the coming of the Paraclete and life under the guidance of the Paraclete.

The coming and the departure are crucial moments in the christological movement of the Fourth Gospel and highlight its basic claim that Jesus is 'the way'. There is a particularity here. There is a universalism as well. As John Painter says: 'Because Jesus is the way, all generations of Christians stand in the same relation to the revelation.'[13] Also, there is a basis for assurance. Jesus paves the way and makes the way known. So, 'Let not your hearts be troubled . . .' (14.1ff.).

Between these crucial moments of coming and departure, descent and ascent, there are smaller comings and goings and actions which are part of the larger revelatory whole. As the good shepherd who knows his sheep, Jesus summons disciples to follow him. As the source of abundant life, Jesus turns water into wine at the wedding feast, offers living water to the woman at the well, makes the lame man walk, heals the official's son, and raises Lazarus from the dead. As the true light, Jesus gives sight to the man born blind. As the one who gives knowledge of true worship, Jesus enacts God's judgment on the temple, goes up to the holy city three times to manifest himself to the people and, as the lamb of God, dies for the sins of the world. Jesus' divinity is manifest in his humanity: in his actions and his death.[14] These are the focus of Christian remembering (cf. 2.22) and the basis in history for a distinctive christocentric spirituality.

4. This brings us to a fourth major aspect of Johannine spirituality: it is a spirituality *bound up with history* and expressing a particular interpretation of history. This point is important because some have claimed that John's gospel represents an escape from history, a retrograde turning aside from the mundane and the material, the societal and the political, in favour of a privatized and pietistic faith.[15] Against such a view, the following observations are particularly pertinent.

First, the account of the trial of Jesus can be seen as a profound and moving attempt to show how to live the life of faith in a society under foreign imperial occupation.[16] It is hardly coincidental that this evangelist alone focuses solely on the trial of Jesus before Pilate (18.28–19.16) and gives no account of a trial before the sanhedrin.[17] At the trial, the leaders of the Jews are shown adopting the politics of expediency (as earlier, at 11.47ff.) and accommodation, which leads to a position of capitulation and apostasy: '"We have no king but Caesar"' (19.15). Jesus, in sharp contrast, bears faithful witness to a kingship 'not of this world', of eternal reality and ultimate authority, opposed to the politics of force (18.36), and in the service of which no compromise or accommodation is possible. This is hardly a form of pious escapism. It is the stuff of martyrdom: and Jesus is crucified for it.[18]

Second, John's gospel shows a pervasive awareness of the cost of discipleship for the believer's historical existence. For Jesus, the divine Word, it means not being received by 'his own' (1.11), having 'no honour in his own country' (4.44), not being believed in even by his own brothers (7.5), and attracting the mortal enmity of the leaders of both the Jews and the Romans. The Passion of Jesus comes, not just at the end of the gospel: rather, the evangelist has taken major elements of the passion tradition and woven them back into the story of Jesus as a whole.[19] The temple cleansing comes in chapter 2, the eucharistic elements of the last supper come in chapter 6, the decision to put Jesus to death is linked to the raising of Lazarus in chapter 11 (at vv. 45–53), the anointing of Jesus at Bethany takes place before the triumphal entry (12.1–8), and a reminiscence of the agony in the garden comes before the last supper, in 12.27–8. The effect of this is to make the gospel as a whole a gospel of the passion. The coming of Jesus provokes conflict and division from the beginning. Likewise, believing in Jesus provokes conflict and division from the beginning.

That is clear from the story of the healing of the man born blind, in chapter 9.[20] From beginning to end, there is an underlying irony. The ones who should be able to see are blind, while the one who is blind comes to full sight. The man's neighbours are divided and confused, his own parents distance themselves from him, the Pharisees and the Jews repeatedly deny

121

the truth of the man's witness to Jesus and finally excommunicate him from the synagogue (v. 34b; cf. v. 22). A story like this is hardly the stuff of privatized, escapist religion. The man's whole being in history is involved: his body, his family and neighbourhood ties, his belonging to the community of the synagogue, and his relations with figures of traditional authority in the community. Believing in Jesus clearly generated very definite historical and existential issues for the believer and for the groups and communities to which he or she belonged, issues which are addressed quite explicitly (cf. 16.1–4). Nils Dahl puts it well: 'What is present in the time after the ascension was anticipated in the life of Jesus, and the witness borne to his historical ministry is, therefore, at the same time a testimony to his presence here and now.'[21]

What the gospel says about 'the world' is a third element important for this aspect of Johannine spirituality.[22] Certainly, 'the world' is viewed in pessimistic and even dualistic terms in John, especially in the second half of the gospel which emphasizes the negative response of humankind to revelation (cf. 1.10; 7.7; 14.17, 22, 27, 30; 15.18f.; 16.8, 20, 33; 17.6, 9, 14ff.). Nevertheless, as Barrett points out, 'the world into which he comes is also the scene of the saving mission of Jesus (1.9f.; 3.17, 19; 6.14; 8.26; 10.36; 12.46; 16.28; 17.13, 18; 18.20, 37), and his mission to the world is grounded in the love of God for the world (3.16).'[23] Furthermore, withdrawal of a sectarian kind from 'the world' is resisted explicitly: 'I do not pray that thou shouldst take them out of the world, but that thou shouldst keep them from the evil one' (17.15). Unlike the Qumran separatists who withdrew to the desert, but like the cosmopolitan city-dweller Paul (cf. 1 Cor. 5.9–10), the fourth evangelist is prepared to live with the tensions of his ambivalence towards unregenerate human society, for the sake of bearing witness.

A fourth and final feature which shows the extent to which Johannine spirituality is bound up with history has to do with this gospel's response to Jewish messianism. There can be no doubt that John claims Jesus as the Messiah. This is the witness of Andrew to Simon Peter: '"We have found the Messiah" (which means Christ)' (1.41), at the beginning of the gospel. Likewise, Nathanael confesses: '"You are the King of Israel!"' (1.49). It

Creation + New Creation

is the witness of Jesus himself, in his dialogue with the Samaritan woman (4.25–26). And at the conclusion of the gospel, the evangelist says that he has written his work in order to convince his readers 'that Jesus is the Christ' (20.31). What is important, however, is the way the evangelist shows that the Christian understanding of the term 'Christ' is different to the Jewish understanding.[24] To the Jews, the messiah is a political warrior king (cf. 6.15; 11.47–8; 19.12) of the Davidic line (7.41–2). According to John, Jesus is messiah because he comes 'from above' rather than from Bethlehem, 'where David was'; because he comes to David's city peacefully and in humility (12.12ff.) rather than as a warrior (18.36); because he faithfully bears witness to the truth (18.37); because, as the kingly shepherd of his people, he lays down his life of his own accord to save them (10.11–18; 11.49–50); and because his death brings salvation, not only to Jews, but to 'the world'. To reinforce the latter point, John tells us that the titulus, which read '"Jesus of Nazareth, the King of the Jews"', was written in Hebrew, Latin and Greek (19.20).

Such a transformation of traditional messianism has undoubted social, ethical and political corollaries and involves the transformation of spirituality as well. Above all, it means that John moves away from an apocalyptic spirituality and a political-military messianism; and that he moves towards a personal, mystical and universalist spirituality based upon the hidden and eternal messiahship of Jesus.

5. If Johannine spirituality is bound up integrally with history, as I have tried to show just now, how does John help his readers to live the life of faith within the sphere of historical existence? If John is a gospel for tough times, as D. Moody Smith maintains,[25] does it encourage *a spirituality for tough times* as well? I think it does, and in two ways. The first has to do with assurance; the second, with perseverance.

First, the gospel provides *grounds for assurance*. This has many facets. Theologically, assurance comes in the revelation of God's love for the world in the sending of his Son, and in the revelation of God's sovereignty in the divine election of a new people of God—the sheep whom Jesus knows by name and whom Jesus calls. Christologically, grounds for assurance come in the presentation of Jesus as exclusively the way to the Father and as the one who, in his own life, death and resurrection, overcame the world and 'the ruler of this world' (12.31). In terms of eschatology, grounds for assurance come in the revelation that judgment and salvation have come *already*, in the person of Jesus the Christ, and that eternal life is available *now* to all who believe in him (13.16–18).

In terms of history, the gospel provides assurance in the form of witnesses. The Father witnesses to the Son (12.28). Jesus the Son witnesses to the Father. After Jesus' departure, the Paraclete/Spirit witnesses to both the Father and the Son (16.7–15). During Jesus' ministry, John bears witness to him; disciples, potential followers and even enemies (like Pilate) bear witness; the scriptures, the patriarchs and the prophets are called upon as witnesses; and the miracles which Jesus does are 'signs' which witness also to Jesus' glory.

In terms of epistemology, the gospel provides a doctrine of knowing[26] particularly conducive of a sense of assurance. For John, saving knowledge is available in the revelation of the Father by the Son. As Jesus says to the Jews, in chapter 8: '"If you continue in my word, you are truly my disciples, and you will know the truth, and the truth will make you free"' (vv. 31–2). Jesus is the Word from God, and Jesus' words invariably begin with a revelatory *amen, amen*.[27] To know the Son is to know the Father (e.g. 14.7); and such knowing is available to anyone who believes in Jesus, whether they have seen him in the flesh, or not (cf. 20.29).

In terms of personal experience, the gospel provides grounds for assurance in the stories of the many individuals, both men and women, from within Israel and outside it, who encounter, in Jesus, the truth. Hear, for example, the confession of Andrew: '"We have found the Messiah"' (1.41). Hear the Samaritan woman: '"Come see a man who told me all that I ever did. Can this be the Christ?"' (4.29). Hear also the man born blind: '"Whether he is a sinner, I do not know; one thing I know, that though I was blind, now I see"' (9.25). Indeed, the gospel represents itself as springing out of the assurance which comes from personal experience. Note the use of the first person in the prologue: 'And the Word became flesh and dwelt *among us* . . .

We have beheld his glory . . . And from his fullness *have we all received*, grace upon grace' (1.14–16).[28] Part of the compelling appeal of John's gospel to Everyperson is the way it speaks with assurance to the reader's own personal experience and offers, in fact, a new quality of personal experience: '. . . that believing you may have life in his name' (20.31).

As well as grounds for assurance, the Fourth Gospel also provides a *basis for perseverance*. In its historical context, we can see why this was needed: the believers were facing persecution, excommunication from the synagogues, and martyrdom (16.1–4; cf. 9.22, 34; 12.42).[29] Such pressures, together with the passage of time and aspects of the believers' own faith, made them prone to disunity, faction and falling away. Again, John's attempt to address such problems and to encourage perseverance has many facets.

Most important is the memory and the remembering of the perseverance of Jesus. Note especially how the second half of the gospel begins: '. . . having loved his own who were in the world, he loved them to the end (*eis telos*)' (13.1). And on the cross, the final word of Jesus is '"It is finished (*tetelestai*)"' (19.30). Jesus does not 'fall away'. He remains faithful to the end and completes his divinely-appointed task. In this, he is a model for his followers.

Another basis for perseverance comes in the prolonged preparation for the departure and absence of Jesus. There is a strong anticipation of this motif in the story of the blind man (ch.9), where one of the most noticeable features of the plot is that Jesus is there in person only at the beginning and at the end. In between, the blind man is forced to bear witness on his own; and his perseverance in so doing brings, not only fierce opposition, but also the reward of final illumination.

But the main preparation comes in the uniquely Johannine 'farewell discourses', in chapters 13–17, set in the context of the last supper. These chapters have all the poignancy and betwixt-and-between tension of a farewell. In biblical terms, they remind us of the farewell speeches of Moses to the people of Israel (Deut. 32–34), and of Paul to the elders at Ephesus (Acts 20.17–38). Here, rather than instituting a eucharistic 'sacrament', Jesus gives teaching, by action and by word, oriented around problems likely to arise after he is with them no longer.

125

The teaching by action consists of the symbolic act of foot-washing whereby Jesus demonstrates the kind of other-regarding love and status-subverting hospitality which is to be the mark of the community of his followers: 'I have given you an example, that you also should do as I have done to you' (13.15).[30] If competition for rank and status in the community of believers was likely to develop after Jesus' death, this episode would function as an important corrective. It is unlikely to be coincidental that not even an apostle like Peter is allowed exceptional treatment (13.6ff.). All alike are bound by the example of the servant-lord (13.13ff.).

The teaching by word includes, first, prophecies of betrayal (13.21–30) and denial (13.36–38) amongst Jesus' own intimates, intended to show that, on God's side, the divine sovereignty is not captive to human frailty, and that, on the part of believers, faithful persistence is required. Second, there is the interpretation by Jesus of his coming death as a departure for the purpose of preparing a place for followers who believe in him (14.1ff.). So Jesus' coming death is not anomic and meaningless, but for a salvific purpose known and revealed in advance. Third, there is the promise that Jesus' departure is necessary, for it will enable the sending of 'another Paraclete' to be with them, comfort them, teach them, and empower them to 'even greater' works (14.12ff.). Fourth, Jesus gives the 'new commandment' to love one another, thus providing a basis for building up the solidarity of the community, overcoming tendencies towards faction, and resisting 'the world'. Fifth, there is the comforting revelation of how things stand in the spiritual realm: that, though 'the ruler of this world is coming', he has no power over Jesus (14.30), and is, in fact, judged already (16.11). Sixth, there is the repeated assurance that Jesus' departure is only 'for a little while', and that believers will see him again (16.16ff.). In this way, the problem of Jesus' departure in death is foreshortened. Seventh, there is the teaching on the efficacy of praying in the name of Jesus (16.23ff.), teaching which reaches a climax in the prayer of Jesus himself to the Father for sanctification in the truth of the elect (ch.17).

The Johannine symbolism is another element of the gospel well suited to the task of encouraging perseverance. J.H. Schütz is right when he says: 'John's images tend toward sustenance and intensification rather than toward growth by extension.'[31] One thinks immediately of the images of light, bread, water, the vine and the branches, and the good shepherd and his sheep, all major images of life-giving sustenance in John, and all of which are intended to encourage a deepening of the relationship between the believer and Christ. It is noticeable, that these images are drawn from the sphere of the everyday, of what is fundamental at the material level for life and the sustaining of life. It is this which makes them so powerful as symbols of what is fundamental for the sustaining of life at the spiritual level, something which is reinforced by the fact that these images are fundamental biblical images as well.

What is noticeable also is the way in which John's use of symbolism affects the interpretation of the 'sacraments'—or, perhaps better, the rites—of baptism and eucharist.[32] As is well known, John gives no account of the baptism of Jesus, no commission to baptize, and no account of the institution of the eucharist. What is important primarily for John is not the rites themselves. So, for instance, a contrast is made between John's water baptism and Jesus' baptism with the Spirit (1.31, 33). What is important for the evangelist is being born from above (and therefore, being born of the Spirit), believing in Jesus as the Christ, and bearing witness to the truth. The rite of baptism loses its exclusive function. As John Painter says: 'Jesus is the *giver* of the life-giving water, and *drinking* is a symbolic description of believing, 6.35. The water which Jesus gives is the life-giving Spirit, 7.37ff. Water is used as a symbol because of its fundamental significance for human life. It is not to be understood in terms of baptism as the reference to *drinking* shows.'[33]

Similarly with the eucharist. Once again, the ritual aspect is subordinated to John's wider symbolic, christological interest. What is important is believing in Jesus as the one who, by his death, gives true, spiritual life. The eating and drinking are metaphors of believing: '"I am the bread of life; he who *comes to me* shall not hunger; and he who *believes in* me shall never thirst"' (6.35). Ingesting Jesus' flesh and blood is not some form of ritual cannibalism (6.52ff.): rather, it is a very powerful (because shocking) metaphor of spiritual union and abiding: '"He who eats my flesh and drinks my blood abides in me (*en emoi menei*) and I in him"' (6.56). The evangelist persistently

127

draws attention away from eucharistic ritual itself to Jesus and especially to *the words* of Jesus as the source of life (6.63–4, 68–9). This is not to say, along with Bultmann and others, that John's gospel is anti-sacramental: only that the rites of baptism and eucharist are seen, neither as ends in themselves, nor as exclusive in function, but as instances of a wider christocentric symbolism designed to evoke a deep, intense and persistent faith in Jesus the revealer.

To such symbolism we must add John's preference for what Margaret Pamment has called 'path and residence metaphors'.[34] We must add also certain distinctive instances of word usage: in particular, John's consistent preference for the verbal forms, *pisteuein* ('to believe') and *menein* ('to remain', 'to abide'). Taken together, these show again how great is the evangelist's concern to encourage a stability of conviction and a strengthening of perseverance on the basis of a lively sense of personal relationship with the Father mediated through the Son.

Yet another aspect of the gospel to encourage a spirituality of perseverance is the characterization, by means of which the evangelist is able to present a kind of typology of faith. The story of Judas Iscariot, for example, is a serious warning against falling away and, at the same time, falling under the control of Satan. The sign that he is not one of Jesus' 'own' is his preoccupation with things material (12.4–6). His fate is catastrophic: 'Satan entered into him' (13.27); and he ends up on the side of Jesus' enemies (18.2ff.).

Nicodemus is characterized by ambiguity.[35] Although he comes to Jesus, he comes at night (3.2). Although he confesses Jesus to be a 'teacher come from God', he himself remains 'a teacher of Israel' who does not understand what Jesus says (3.10–12). Although he is there at the end, his terms of reference remain within Jewish custom: the duty of the pious to bury the dead (19.39ff.). He seems to represent an inadequate type of faith: the sympathetic, even pious, follower, whose recognition of Jesus is limited, remains at the earthly level and, therefore, is not to be trusted. The narrator's comment in 2.23–25, immediately prior to the introduction of Nicodemus, confirms this verdict.

Thomas is a person whose faith has not matured in such a way as to require no longer tangible, material signs: ' "Unless I see in his hands the print of the nails, and place my finger in the mark of the nails, and place my hand in his side, I will not believe"' (20.25). Even though his emphatic[36] ultimatum is graciously met, and he comes uniquely to confess Jesus as God (20.28), the beatitude is pronounced by the risen One upon others: '"Blessed are those who have not seen and yet believe"' (20.29). For the fourth evangelist, physical signs (and likewise ritual action) may be important, but only in a qualified way: as aids towards the practice of a mature faith which accepts Jesus on the basis of his word or 'commandment' alone.

Then there is that uniquely Johannine figure, the beloved disciple. Introduced for the first time at the last supper (13.23ff.), he seems to function for the evangelist as the antithesis of Judas and the epitome of the true believer. Note the evangelist's emphasis on his closeness to Jesus (13.23, 25; and cf. 21.20). The phrase used of the relation of the beloved disciple to Jesus—*en to kolpo tou Iesou* (lit. 'in the bosom of Jesus')—is reminiscent of the description of the relation of Jesus to the Father, in 1.18 (*eis ton kolpon tou patros*—'in the bosom of the Father'.)[37] So this disciple's relationship of personal intimacy with Jesus is analogous to that of Jesus with the Father, a pattern of which Jesus himself specifically speaks, in 14.20–1: '"In that day you will know that I am in my Father, and you in me, and I in you. He who has my commandments and keeps them, he it is who loves me; and he who loves me will be loved by my Father, and I will love him and manifest myself to him."' A subsequent mention of this disciple finds him, yet again, in close relationship with Jesus, standing at the foot of the cross with Jesus' mother. His relationship of love for Jesus is perduring, unlike that of Peter; and, in reward, he is made a member of Jesus' spiritual family, and takes the mother of Jesus to his own home (19.26–7). But the beloved disciple is present, not only at the last supper and at the cross. He is present at the empty tomb, as well; and of him specifically (and not Peter), it is said that 'he saw and believed' (20.8). So his function in the story is that he interprets correctly—that is, with faith—the significance of the empty tomb. Likewise later, it is he who recognizes Jesus by the Sea of Tiberias, and says to Peter, '"It is the Lord!"' (21.7). As Raymond Brown points out, 'Faith is possible for the Beloved Disciple because he has become very sensitive to Jesus through love. . . . The lesson for the reader is that love for Jesus gives one the insight to detect his presence. The Beloved Disciple, here as elsewhere the ideal follower of Jesus, sets an example for all others who would follow.'[38]

We could look at other characters in the Johannine narrative in the same kind of way, but enough has been said to show that the characters have a representative quality, allowing the evangelist to explore what are the marks of the true believer and what qualities are required for personal faith in Jesus to endure. The message that comes through loud and clear is that Christian spirituality according to John demands perseverance. It is rooted in believing in Jesus alone, and abiding in a relationship of reciprocal love with him, and through him with the Father.

6. The kind of spirituality which results from this believing and abiding in Jesus is a spirituality appropriately described as *charismatic*. By this I mean that belief in the power of the eschatological Spirit and experiences of the presence of the Spirit in the life of the church are a very important feature of Johannine Christianity. This should not surprise us. It has long been recognized that the primitive church generally was a charismatic movement. Pauline Christianity likewise, as J.D.G. Dunn amongst others has shown.[39] But the charismatic dimension of Johannine spirituality has not, perhaps, been recognized sufficiently.

We note, first, that Jesus is depicted in charismatic terms. The Spirit descends from heaven and remains (*menein*) on him (1.32, 33). He it is who baptizes with the Holy Spirit (1.33). He it is who, uniquely, has seen God (cf. 1.18; 3.11–13, 31ff.) and therefore reveals the truth about God and the way to God.[40] When God speaks, as he does only once in John, he speaks in response to the prayer of Jesus (12.27–8). Throughout the narrative, Jesus exercises prophetic powers (e.g. 1.47ff.; 2.19–22; 4.16–19, 44, 50–4; 9.17; 11.1ff.; etc.); he performs extraordinary miracles to the extent even of raising a man from the dead; his teaching comes in the form of revelatory oracles claiming divine authority; he shows throughout an awareness of a uniquely intimate relationship with God as his Father and claims to mediate the relationship between God and the world (14.6); and at the end, he himself is raised from the dead and becomes a heavenly traveller, ascending back to the Father (20.17; cf. 17.11ff.).

Because Jesus is the one who baptizes with the Holy Spirit (1.33; 3.34), his followers who believe in him are depicted in charismatic terms also. In a quite specific sense, the gospel of John is addressed to charismatic disciples, those who have received the Spirit now that Jesus has been glorified (cf. 7.39; 20.22). This is important for our study of Johannine spirituality.

It means, for instance, that the life of faith is seen as a response to God's sovereign grace to the individual who has been born 'of the Spirit' (3.5ff.). A corollary of this is that the life of faith is *not mediated* by family or patriarch or calendar or cult or holy place. But this does not mean that the relationship with God is not mediated at all, and that the believer has *direct* access to the Father—a doctrine which may lie behind both the gospel and the Johannine epistles and to which their teaching is a response.[41] On the contrary, for the evangelist, it *is* mediated, and it is mediated by Jesus who alone is 'the way' (14.6), and by the Spirit whom Jesus sends to continue the work which he has accomplished. So any anomic tendencies arising out of a doctrine of spiritual regeneration which undercuts law and cult are circumscribed carefully in John by the overwhelming emphasis on Jesus as the way, on doing the commandments of Jesus and following his example (e.g. 13.12–17), and on the Spirit as the one who continues *Jesus'* work as *'another* Paraclete' (14.16).[42]

Furthermore, possession of the Spirit gives believers power. This power is spiritual power, not traditional or bureaucratic or material or military or based upon race or gender. It gives access to, and is based upon, esoteric knowledge, a kind of hidden wisdom which is not of this world but comes by revelation of the Spirit (cf. 14.26; 16.12–15) and is opaque to outsiders.[43] Nicodemus discovers this to his cost: 'Jesus answered him, ". . . If I have told you earthly things (*ta epigeia*) and you do not believe, how can you believe if I tell you heavenly things (*ta epourania*)?"' (3.10–12). So also does Pilate: 'Jesus answered, "My kingship is not of this world; if my kingship were of this world, my servants would fight . . . but my kingship is not from the world"' (18.36ff.). This alternative source of power, which is at the same time an alternative interpretation of power, makes possible resistance to the powers-that-be, and the subversion of normative power relations—something about which the Sanhedrin and Caiaphas, for example, show particular concern, after the raising of Lazarus, in chapter 11.

It also makes possible *the transformation of the old community and its members into the new*. This transformation happens in a number of ways. First, there is a charismatic foreshortening of traditional eschatological perspectives, such that believers in Jesus become *already* inheritors of eternal life, pass from death to life and from darkness to light, and become recipients of the eschatological Spirit. This novel eschatological doctrine has the effect of separating those who hold to it from those who do not. Either Jesus is the longed-for messiah or he is not; either 'the hour' has come or it has not; either the 'ruler of this world' has been expelled for ever from the court of heaven or he has not; either eternal life and the gifts of the Spirit are available now or they are not. In other words, the radical foreshortening of traditional eschatological perspectives provides the legitimation for the formation of a new kind of solidarity, separate from the old.

Second, there is a charismatic-prophetic reinterpretation of the scriptures and of traditional salvation history. Now, the scriptures and the patriarchs[44] are understood as bearing witness against the people of God traditionally conceived and to Jesus alone: '"You search the scriptures, because you think that in them you have eternal life; and it is they that bear witness to me. . . . Do not think that I shall accuse you to the Father; it is Moses who accuses you, on whom you set your hope. If you believed Moses, you would believe me, for he wrote of me"' (5.39ff.). Note that this reinterpretation of scripture is not really argued exegetically. Rather, it is asserted as new revelation given by Jesus, which those who are born 'from above' will accept, and those who judge 'according to the flesh' (8.15) will not understand.

Third, the teaching of Jesus in the gospel represents the institution of a new, transcendental understanding of worship 'in spirit and truth' (4.23–4). Now, the temple is the resurrected body of Jesus (2.19–22), and Jesus is the sacrificial lamb (1.29). Now, given a radical emphasis on God as Spirit (4.24) and on the believer as born of the Spirit (3.6), true worship is inward and translocal, and not dependent on the cult or on the traditional holy places or on the traditional mediators of grace. Now, prayer is a matter of every believer asking the Father in the name of Jesus (e.g. 14.13, 14; 15.16; 16.23, 24, 26f.). There is no set form (not even the Lord's Prayer!), and there is no sacerdotal paraphernalia. Even spiritual discernment and discipline become matters for the Christian fellowship itself rather than, as traditionally, for the priesthood and the Sanhedrin (cf. 20.22–3), who, in any case, show themselves to be spiritually blind in a most disastrous way.

Finally, we may mention the exercise of a charismatic ministry of healing. This is made explicit for the post-resurrection period, in 14.12f.: '"Truly, truly, I say to you, he who believes in me will also do the works that I do; and greater works than these will he do, because I go to the Father. Whatever you ask in my name, I will do it . . ."'. What these 'works' are is not made plain, but it is fair to assume that they include the working of miraculous cures on the sick. After all, the first half of the gospel has depicted Jesus as a worker of miraculous signs of which the disciples are witnesses, and these works continue into the post-resurrection period (21.4–8). Also, the evangelist clearly believes that miracles have evidential value as grounds for faith (14.11; 20.30–1). If they constituted part of the mission of Jesus, they are most likely to constitute part of the mission of his disciples as well (cf. 17.18). In addition, we know from other New Testament writings that the followers of Jesus were charismatic miracle workers (cf. Matt. 21.21; Mark 16.17–18; Acts, *passim*; etc.). Nevertheless, it is interesting, as Brown points out,[45] that John does not emphasize the marvellous character of the 'greater works' to be performed by the disciples. For him, what is of overriding importance is the believing and abiding in Jesus that makes such 'works' possible (14.12a), together with the fact that the goal of the 'works' is the glory of the Father in the Son (14.13).

Conclusion

The preceding reflections hardly do justice to our subject. Much more needs to be said and further attention could be given to the work of other writers on the subject of Johannine spirituality.[46] But it is necessary now to bring the discussion to a conclusion by making some observations of a more critical and evaluative kind

133

and by opening up areas where further exploration might be helpful.

One feature of Johannine spirituality which comes as a surprise is something which is noticeably lacking. *There is very little ethics.*[47] If we interrogate the Fourth Gospel for teaching on how to live now in the light of the revelation of God incarnate, the answer we get is emphatic enough but curiously unelaborated. Whereas in the synoptics, Jesus is depicted teaching and debating in public about personal and social morality, about questions relating to customary observances and issues to do with the conduct of everyday life—marriage and divorce, the payment of taxes, relations with civil authorities, the practice of lending and borrowing, the swearing of oaths, sabbath observance, and the like—the Jesus of the Fourth Gospel gives no such public instruction. Another way of putting this is to say that there is no sermon on the mount in John. Instead, all we find is teaching of a very general kind in private to the disciples: the teaching of the 'new commandment' of brotherly love and the obligation to 'go and bear fruit' (cf. 15.12–17). Whereas in Matthew, Moses and the Torah remain critically important for guidance in the way of righteousness (cf. Matt. 5.17–19), in John they are important only in the witness they bear to Jesus as 'the way' (cf. 5.39–47).

What are we to make of this? Perhaps it is the case that John takes for granted the moral tradition of Israel which he has inherited in the scriptures. So when Jesus says 'that you should go and bear fruit and that your fruit should abide' (15.16a), he and his readers know that this is done by living according to Torah. Certainly, however, this is not made explicit in the way it is in Matthew, for example. Indeed, the tendency in John is to displace alternative mediators of the knowledge of the will of God such as Moses. The tendency also is to relativize and reinterpret Torah, the observance of the sabbath being a particular case in point (cf. 5.18; note also 7.19–24).

Perhaps, then, it is the case that moral instruction and Christian casuistry are understood as unnecessary. Perhaps the relation of the believer to Jesus is so intense and intimate—that of the 'friend' (*philos*) rather than of the 'servant' or 'slave' (*doulos*), according to 15.13–15—that knowing how to act will come by direct revelation, springing out of the mutual abiding of the child of God and the Son of God with the Father. Perhaps, to put it another way, Christian ethics according to John is fundamentally charismatic, a matter of total dependence on the guidance of the Spirit-Paraclete, of whom Jesus says, 'he will guide you into all the truth' (16.13).

If these suggestions about Johannine ethics have any merit, then certain concerns are worth voicing. First, there is the danger that a community which lives according to the ethic, 'love one another', where the 'other' is one's fellow believer, is likely to turn in upon itself in a way which is claustrophobic and narcissistic. On the other hand, in a context where the tendency towards disunity is strong, such an ethic has an obvious place. Furthermore, it is probably true to say that the centripetal tendencies of the Johannine love ethic are counterbalanced in a healthy way by the affirmation of the love of God for the world and by the obvious concern for mission to the world, of which the story of Jesus and the woman of Samaria in 4.1–42 is so paradigmatic.[48]

Second, it is questionable whether the overwhelming concentration on christology and the apparently minimalist approach to ethics in the Fourth Gospel are able to provide a satisfactory basis for the maintenance of a common Christian life, in touch with daily affairs and able to relate to the world at large. Certainly, separation from the world appears to have been a tendency—hence the prayer of Jesus: 'I do not pray that thou shouldst take them out of the world . . .' (17.15a). Numerous scholars, furthermore, have argued recently that the Fourth Gospel betrays a bias towards sectarianism, a strong ethos of 'us' over against 'them', where it is natural to be most concerned about delineating the boundaries and where less attention is given to how to live within (or beyond) the boundaries.[49] If this is so, then the adequacy of the spiritual vision of John for the life of faith in the mundane, everyday world of family life, politics and economics may leave something to be desired. For help in these areas, the synoptics are more obvious places to go, as are Paul's letters, the Pastoral epistles and 1 Peter.

From questions about ethics, we should broach another important area of concern about the adequacy of Johannine spirituality—namely, its *intense particularity and exclusiveness*. Jesus,

135

as the Son of God and incarnate Word, is the only way to the Father. He alone is 'the way, the truth, and the life' (14.6). At the climax of the prologue, a massive gulf is fixed between Moses and the old dispensation, on the one hand, and Jesus and the new dispensation, on the other: 'For the law was given through Moses; grace and truth came through Jesus Christ' (1.17). In fact, the law is now referred to by Jesus as *your* law' or *'their* law' (e.g. 8.17; 10.34; 15.25), so great is the sense of alienation from the tradition and its guardians. All the traditional symbols of revelation and salvation are transferred to Jesus. He bears the divine *doxa* ('glory'), he is the atoning lamb, he makes the eschatological wine freely available, his body is the temple, he is the Word of God and the Wisdom of God, he bestows the eschatological Spirit, and so on. And the corollary of this intense concentration of revelatory and soteriological symbols on Jesus is a thorough-going denuding of Judaism and a vilification of those who are referred to as 'the Jews'. Says Jesus to the Jews, in what is perhaps the most vitriolic exchange of the gospel: 'You are of your father the devil, and your will is to do your father's desires. He was a murderer from the beginning, and has nothing to do with the truth, because there is no truth in him' (8.44).

It is difficult to respond to the particularity and exclusivism of John in a balanced way. Indeed, a 'balanced' response is not always what is appropriate. Nevertheless, it should be said that particularity and exclusivism are characteristics not at all unique to Johannine Christianity. Ironically, they are characteristics inherited from the religion of Israel and from the scriptures of Israel and which continue to be features of various sects and parties within the Judaism of the time of Jesus and the fourth evangelist.[50] Thus, there is a sense in which the particularity and exclusivism of John is thoroughly explicable in its historical situation. It mirrors the same characteristics of the (often rather heterodox)[51] Judaism with which it has so much in common and from which it has separated and been separated so violently. What is more, the persecution of believers to which the gospel adverts more than once (cf. 15.18ff.; 16.1–4) will not have done anything to encourage a more ecumenical mentality on the believers' part. Like many family quarrels, the intimacy of the protagonists will have made the separation and mutual antagonism all the greater.

So Johannine particularity and exclusivism are understandable religiously, historically and sociologically. If they offend modern, 'liberal' sympathies of one kind or another, it is in part at least because liberal sympathies are a factor of modernity—at least in some quarters!—and it is anachronistic to expect the same sympathies to pervade antiquity, even Christian antiquity.

Nevertheless, it is important to see what there is that is positive about this feature of Johannine spirituality. On the one hand, it is important to give full recognition to the claim of the gospel itself that the belief in the uniqueness of Christ springs from the believers' *own experience* of him, that the followers of Jesus found in him what they came to describe as 'eternal life', and that this was a spiritual revitalization that they experienced nowhere else. Seen in these terms, the particularity of Johannine christology and soteriology is an expression of what was existentially real for his followers (cf. 1 John 1.1–4).[52] On the other hand, it is important to recognize what the Johannine particularism makes possible—namely, a new universalism and a corresponding redefinition of the people of God. Now that salvation and the way to God are defined in terms of relationship to Christ rather than in terms of circumcision, Torah and temple, then access to salvation is opened up in a much more unmediated way to men and women of all nations: 'that *whoever believes in him* should not perish but have eternal life' (3.16). The revolutionary implications of this universalism, springing from the profound sense that the love of God for all humankind is revealed uniquely in Jesus, are difficult to underestimate.

We have reflected critically on the ethics of John and on Johannine particularity and exclusivism. One last area worth consideration is that of *Johannine ecclesiology*. Does John have what we might call an adequate ecclesiology, and if not, is this a serious limitation on his vision of the spiritual life?[53] Certainly, alongside the undoubted appeal to the individual there is a strong sense of the corporate, as I showed earlier. But there are a number of distinctive features of John which may give pause for thought. I have in mind, first, the apparent playing down of ritual in the life of the community in favour of the intensification of the individual member's believing and abiding in Christ. Second, there is the shift of attention away from the apostles, including even Peter, in the direction of a focus upon discipleship in general.[54] Third, there is a tendency towards undifferentiated egalitarianism, combined with a dogmatic emphasis on the availability of the Spirit-Paraclete to each and every believer. Fourth, there seems to be no interest in acknowledging a diversity of spiritual gifts within the community—along the lines, say, of Paul's metaphor of the church as a 'body'. Associated with this, the various issues related to the recognition and distribution of authority in the community appear not to be addressed. Finally, if 'the hour is coming and now is when the true worshippers will worship the Father in spirit and in truth' (4.23), one is left wondering if the disregard for temple, tradition, festivals and religious calendar resulted in a religious vacuum. To put it bluntly, what did the Johannine Christians do when they met together? How did they express the corporate dimension of their spirituality? Does the vacuum in this area help to explain the tendency towards division and faction which comes to the surface in the Johannine epistles (e.g. 1 John 2.18ff.; 4.1–6)?

I do not wish to gainsay what is so important about Johannine spirituality here. If John plays down baptism and eucharist, it is from a sense that the life and death of Jesus is the true and only sacrament and that nothing should detract from abiding in him and following his example of self-giving love (cf. esp. 13.1–20).[55] If John shifts attention away from the apostles, it is from a conviction that the believer in Jesus in the period after the apostles is at no disadvantage. He or she is not dependent on them, because the Spirit-Paraclete indwells every believer and it is the Spirit who bears witness to Christ. If John pays little attention to the ordering of authority, it is from the belief that eternal life is available to all and that traditional mediations of religious power—including the cultic and the patriarchal—have been displaced irrevocably. The question which remains from the perspective of later generations, however, must be whether or not John's exalted vision is strong enough and durable enough and flexible enough to make possible its own routinization, both in the daily life and worship of the believing community and in the intercourse of the church with the world.

How shall we conclude an investigation into the spirituality of the Fourth Gospel? Perhaps we do best to take our cue from the final chapter of the gospel itself. This is how the gospel ends: 'But there are also many other things which Jesus did; were every one of them to be written, I suppose that the world itself could not contain the books that would be written' (21.25). This is suggestive, not least at the level of spirituality. Above all, it suggests that coming to know Jesus is the most important thing in the world, and that this is a never-ending process. The Fourth Gospel may give us all that we need to know about Jesus, but it does not give us all that it is possible to know—because, as Ernst Käsemann says, Jesus 'is always greater than his witnesses and reporters'.[56] Knowing what John says about Jesus is no substitute for coming to know Jesus personally and abiding in him as the way to the Father. Put a little more academically, we may say that theology is not the same thing as personal faith, even if the two belong together.[57] Knowing Jesus personally is an experience open to men and women of every historical epoch; and John's gospel concludes in this open-ended way in order to invite ever new encounters with Jesus. That is how the tradition of faith grows and is made contemporary: by the witness borne to Jesus by those to whom he comes and who come to him in the present.

The final chapter of John also tells us what Jesus asks of those who believe in him. It is the question which Jesus puts three times to Peter: '"Do you love me?"' *That* is what lies at the heart of Christian spirituality: simple, total love of Jesus. And lest such love of Jesus become a private, individual obsession, Jesus lays upon Peter an obligation: '"Feed my sheep"' (21.17). This is a serious obligation. It will cost Peter his life (21.18–19), just as it cost the Good Shepherd his. But that is the way of the Christian in the world. Love of Jesus can never be a private escape. It is bound up always with the church and with the world, out of love for which God sent his Son.

Notes

1. On the interpretation of John in the patristic period, see M.F. Wiles, *The Spiritual Gospel: The Interpretation of the Fourth Gospel in the Early Church* (Cambridge: Cambridge University Press, 1960).
2. On the theological implications of the anonymity of the author of

THE SPIRITUALITY OF THE GOSPELS

the Fourth Gospel, see B.S. Childs, *The New Testament as Canon: An Introduction* (London: SCM Press, 1984), pp. 128–30.

3. See further, J.D.G. Dunn, *Christology in the Making* (London: SCM Press, 1980), pp. 56–9.

4. See further, R.F. Collins, 'The Representative Figures of the Fourth Gospel', *Downside Review*, 94 (1976), pp. 26–46, 118–32.

5. Note the comment of J.D.G. Dunn, 'Models of Christian Community in the New Testament', in D. Martin and P. Mullen, eds., *Strange Gifts? A Guide to Charismatic Renewal* (Oxford: Blackwell, 1984), p. 13: 'John seems to understand Christianity as much more an individual affair, the immediacy of the disciple's relationship with Christ through the Spirit who constitutes Christ's continuing presence in the believer (John 14:15–20; 1 John 3:24).'

6. See, e.g., S. Kierkegaard, *Attack Upon 'Christendom'* (ET, Princeton: Princeton University Press, 1968).

7. See further, F.F. Segovia, *Love Relationships in the Johannine Tradition* (Chico: Scholars Press, 1982); D. Rensberger, *Johannine Faith and Liberating Community* (London: SPCK. 1989); also, S.C. Barton, 'The Communal Dimension of Earliest Christianity', *Journal of Theological Studies* (1992, forthcoming).

8. On the gender-inclusiveness of John, see further, R.E. Brown, *The Community of the Beloved Disciple* (London: Chapman, 1979), pp. 183–98; also, S.C. Barton, 'Women, Jesus and the Gospels', in R. Holloway, ed., *Who Needs Feminism? Men Respond to Sexism in the Church* (London: SPCK, 1991), pp. 48–54.

9. Cf. M. de Jonge on 'The Son of God and the Children of God', in his *Jesus: Stranger from Heaven* (Missoula: Scholars Press, 1977), pp. 141–68.

10. Cf. D.B. Woll, *Johannine Christianity in Conflict* (Chico: Scholars Press, 1981) for an important exploration of the theme of unity in the farewell discourse.

11. See further, J. Painter, *John: Witness & Theologian* (London: SPCK, 1975), pp. 37–49.

12. Using the I AM form, Jesus identifies himself as 1. the bread of life (6.35, 41, 48), 2. the light of the world (8.12; 9.5), 3. the door (10.7, 9), 4. the good shepherd (10.11, 14), 5. the resurrection and the life (11.25), 6. the way, the truth, and the life (14.6), and 7. the true vine (15.1, 5).

13. Painter, *John*, p. 42.

14. See further, M.M. Thompson, *The Humanity of Jesus in the Fourth Gospel* (Philadelphia: Fortress, 1988).

15. Cf. E. Käsemann, *The Testament of Jesus: A Study of the Gospel of John in the Light of Chapter 17* (ET, London: SCM Press, 1968).

16. See Rensberger, *Community*, ch.5; also, the earlier essay of Heinrich Schlier, 'The State according to the New Testament', in

140

his *The Relevance of the New Testament* (ET, London: Burns & Oates, 1968), pp. 215–38, especially 216–25.

17. Note also the presence of the *Roman* soldiers at the arrest of Jesus, in 18.3, 12.

18. Rensberger's conclusion, in *Community*, pp. 99–100, is worth quoting here: 'The Fourth Gospel, for all its sectarianism and inwardness, does not offer a retreat from political relationships, though the approach to them that it does offer is every bit as radical as its Christology. Indeed, it is just the Johannine alienation from the world that ought to make John's refusal of allegiance to the world's political orders somewhat less than surprising. It was an alienation of consciousness as much as an overtly social one, to be sure, yet precisely as such it could be expected to be realized "in the world" as well. . . . The Fourth Gospel confronts the issue of Israel's freedom in the late first-century Roman Empire with an alternative to both zealotry and collaboration, by calling for adherence to the king who is not of this world, whose servants do not fight but remain in the world bearing witness to the truth before the rulers of both synagogue and Empire.'

19. See Rensberger, *Community*, pp. 75–6.

20. The classic treatment is J.L. Martyn, *History and Theology in the Fourth Gospel* (Nashville: Abingdon, 1979[2]).

21. N. Dahl, 'The Johannine Church and History', in J. Ashton, ed., *The Interpretation of John* (London: SPCK, 1986), p. 126.

22. *Kosmos* occurs 78 times in John, 23 times in 1 John, and only 15 times in the synoptics, according to Painter, *John*, p. 31.

23. Barrett, *John*, p. 161; see also, N.H. Cassem, 'A Grammatical and Contextual Inventory of the Use of *kosmos* in the Johannnine Corpus', *New Testament Studies*, 19 (1972–3), pp. 81–91, at p. 89.

24. Dahl, 'History', p. 127.

25. See D.M. Smith, 'Theology and Ministry in John', in E.E. Shelp and R. Sunderland, eds., *A Biblical Basis for Ministry* (Philadelphia: Westminster, 1981), pp. 186–238, at p. 214.

26. Significantly, the Johannine writings never use the noun, *gnosis*, preferring instead the two verbs *ginoskein* (fifty-six times in John) and *eidenai* (eighty-five times in John). According to R.E. Brown, *The Gospel according to John I-XII* (London: Chapman, 1972), p. 514, there is no sharp distinction in sense between John's usage of the two verbs.

27. The synoptic sayings of Jesus of this form, have only a single *amen*!

28. Cf. also 19.35, which is especially emphatic: 'He who saw it has borne witness—his testimony is true and he knows that he tells the truth—that you also may believe.'

29. Cf. B. Lindars, 'The Persecution of Christians in John 15:18–16:4a', in W. Horbury and B. McNeil, eds., *Suffering and Martyrdom*

    in the New Testament (Cambridge: Cambridge University Press, 1981), pp. 48–69.

30. See further, A.J. Hultgren, 'The Johannine Footwashing (13:1–11) as Symbol of Eschatological Hospitality', *New Testament Studies*, 28 (1982), pp. 539–46; and S.M. Schneider, 'The Footwashing (John 13:1–20): An Experiment in Hermeneutics', *Catholic Biblical Quarterly*, 43 (1981), pp. 76–92.

31. J.H. Schütz, 'Ethos of Early Christianity', in *Interpreters Dictionary of the Bible—Supplementary Volume*, pp. 289–94, at p. 292.

32. Of course, strictly speaking, it is anachronistic to speak of sacraments so far as earliest Christianity is concerned. As C.K. Barrett says, in *The Gospel according to John* (London: SPCK, 1978²), p. 85: 'John . . . like the other New Testament writers, has no word for sacrament, and can therefore hardly be supposed to have a sacramental theology or even a theology of the sacraments . . .'. See also, R.E. Brown, *The Churches the Apostles Left Behind* (New York: Paulist Press, 1984), p. 88, n.126.

33. J. Painter, 'Johannine Symbols: A Case Study in Epistemology', *Journal of Theology for Southern Africa*, 27 (1979), pp. 26–41, at pp. 30–1.

34. M. Pamment, 'Path and Residence Metaphors in the Fourth Gospel', *Theology*, 88 (1985), pp. 118–25.

35. See further, Collins, 'Representative Figures', pp. 36–7; also, J.M. Bassler, 'Mixed Signals: Nicodemus in the Fourth Gospel', *Journal of Biblical Literature*, 108 (1989), pp. 635–46.

36. Note the rhetorical pattern of three, in 20.25, as well as the implicit doubting of the witness of 19.34ff..

37. See R.E. Brown, *The Gospel according to John XIII-XXI* (London: Chapman, 1972), p. 577.

38. Brown, *John XIII-XXI*, p. 1005.

39. See J.D.G. Dunn, *Baptism in the Holy Spirit* (London: SCM Press, 1970); *idem, Jesus and the Spirit* (London: SCM Press, 1975).

40. On the likely influence of Jewish apocalyptic and mystical traditions on the distinctive christology of John, see J.D.G. Dunn, 'Let John be John: A Gospel for its Time', in P. Stuhlmacher, ed., *Das Evangelium und Die Evangelien* (Tübingen: Mohr/Siebeck, 1983), pp. 310–39, esp. pp. 322 ff..

41. See further Woll, *Johannine Christianity*.

42. See most recently, G.M. Burge, *The Anointed Community: The Holy Spirit in the Johannine Tradition* (Grand Rapids: Eerdmans, 1987).

43. Cf. G.W.E. Nickelsburg, 'Revealed Wisdom as a Criterion for Inclusion and Exclusion: From Jewish Sectarianism to Early Christianity', in J. Neusner and E.S. Frerichs, eds., *"To See Ourselves as Others See Us": Christians, Jews, "Others" in Late Antiquity* (Chico: Scholars Press, 1985), pp. 73–91, with pp. 82–3 on the Fourth Gospel.

44. See Dahl, 'History', p. 128. Speaking of the historical figures of the OT, he says: 'The Evangelist rather insists upon their inner-worldly nature; in themselves, isolated from Christ, they are of no redemptive value. . . . Like John the Baptist, the OT fathers and prophets are, in the Fourth Gospel, witnesses to Christ, and that is their only true greatness.'

45. Brown, *John XIII-XXI*, p. 633.

46. See, for example, W.G. Thompson, *The Gospels for your Whole Life: Mark and John in Prayer and Study* (Minneapolis: Winston Press, 1983), Part 2; L.W. Countryman, *The Mystical Way in the Fourth Gospel* (Philadelphia: Fortress, 1987); also, D. McGann, *Journeying Within Transcendence: A Jungian Perspective on the Gospel of John* (London: Collins, 1989).

47. So, too, J.L. Houlden, *Ethics and the New Testament* (London: Mowbray, 1973), pp. 35–41.

48. See further, Teresa Okure, *The Johannine Approach to Mission: A Contextual Study of John 4:1–42* (Tübingen: Mohr/Siebeck, 1988).

49. The classic essay is that of W.A. Meeks, 'The Man from Heaven in Johannine Sectarianism', in J. Ashton, *Interpretation of John*, pp. 141–73; cf. also, D.M. Smith, 'Johannine Christianity: Some Reflections on its Character and Delineation', *New Testament Studies*, 21 (1975), pp. 224–48, esp. pp. 223–4.

50. See further, Nickelsburg, 'Revealed Wisdom'.

51. See further Dunn, 'Let John be John', on the proximity of Johannine thought to ideas in the heterodox Judaism of the first century.

52. Cf. Brown, *Churches*, p. 97: 'I speak of the "mystery" of Jesus' ministry in order to do justice to an element about Jesus' life that escapes discursive description . . . Even very skeptical NT critics will admit that in his life Jesus must have impressed people as extraordinary. But the tone of the following of Jesus in the ministry involves more than that—even more than religious awe and veneration. Jesus was remembered as one who exhibited love in what he did and was loved deeply by those who followed him. Detecting love between Jesus and his disciples is not an aberration of nineteenth-century exegesis . . .'.

53. See further, Brown, *Churches*, chs.6–7.

54. See further, R.E. Brown, *The Community of the Beloved Disciple* (London: Chapman, 1979), pp. 81–8; also, J.S. Siker-Gieseler, 'Disciples and Discipleship in the Fourth Gospel: A Canonical Approach', *Studia Biblica et Theologica*, 10 (1980), pp. 199–227.

55. Cf. Barrett, *John*, p. 82: 'If it is true that the Word became flesh, what room is left for minor manifestations of the divine in the material? Will not the great, the ultimate, sacrament drive out the minor ones?'

56. E. Käsemann, *Jesus Means Freedom* (ET, Philadelphia: Fortress, 1972), p. 151.

57. See, again, Käsemann, *Freedom*, p. 148.

143

CONCLUSION

In the preceding chapters, I have tried to describe and evaluate the spirituality of the four canonical gospels. The main task is done, therefore—at least in so far as I am able to do it. I want now, in conclusion, to address several more general issues, some of which were raised with me when these lectures were delivered originally.

The first issue is this. To what extent does the *spirituality of Jesus* lie behind what we may call the spiritualit*ies* of the gospels? This is a necessary and important question, not least because it springs from the central affirmation of Christian faith that living under the lordship of Christ involves a response to the person of Jesus. If the spiritualities of the gospels have little or no connection with the spirituality of Jesus, then it is impossible to describe them, in any traditional sense at least, as Christian.

Although the question is necessary and important, it is not easy to answer, above all, because we have no testimony to the spirituality of Jesus other than the gospels themselves, together with what we can glean from the rest of the New Testament (e.g. Phil. 2.5–11; Heb. 12.2–3) and other early Christian literature. The gospels themselves provide the best evidence that we have, even though there is an inevitable circularity of argument in using them to see if they accurately reflect, or are legitimate expressions of, the spirituality of Jesus. There is another difficulty, as well. That is the difficulty of discerning Jesus' own sense of the presence of God, Jesus' own God-consciousness—where the danger all the time is to read back our own predispositions and presuppositions into the awareness of Jesus.

There is a sense, then, in which it is necessary to take the gospels *on trust*: which is what the church does in regarding and reading the gospels as scripture. It is certainly valid and necessary to keep awake to the possibility that the gospels at certain points misrepresent the spirituality of Jesus or construe it in an inappropriate way. But that is something quite different from coming to the gospels wholly mistrustful of their re-presentations of Jesus. On the other hand, the weakness in approaching the gospels with too much confidence in the historical accuracy of their accounts is that this approach tends to equate the truth about Jesus with what can be known historically about him. Then, ironically, faith makes itself captive to the canons of secular history. So to take the gospels on trust is not to accept everything that they say at face value as true representations of Jesus. Rather, it is to accept the testimony of the church that reading the gospels is life-giving because the gospels bear witness to the man Jesus who, as the one from God, was—and is—the ultimate giver of life. The critical test of the truth of the gospels about Jesus, therefore, is not historical but communal and practical.[1] The test is the fruits that reading the gospels as testimony to Jesus bear in the life and worship of the community which preserves the gospels, the church.

This, of course, is not a direct answer to the question of the extent to which the spirituality of Jesus lies behind the spiritualities of the gospels. Rather, it is to say that from a traditional Christian point of view, we may take it on trust that it does indeed. The attempt to show that it does would require a different book from this one, on the spirituality of Jesus of Nazareth. A likely outcome of such an inquiry would be that, while a plausible account could be given of the spirituality of Jesus—with attention focusing naturally on the religious resources of the Judaism of Jesus' day, Jesus' sense of vocation, Jesus' attitude to the temple and Torah, Jesus' teaching on prayer and faith, Jesus as charismatic healer and miracle worker, the suffering of Jesus, and so on[2]—the gospel portraits would represent a development in one direction or another of what we found for Jesus. In accepting the four gospels as scripture, the Christian community of faith has affirmed, and continues to affirm, that these portraits represent developments in understanding Jesus which are legitimate and, taken together, fundamentally life-giving.

It is important, however, that the gospel portraits of Jesus and the life of faith be *taken together*. This brings me to a second general issue about the spirituality of the gospels which deserves

145

attention—namely, the significance of the fact that the Christian canon of scripture contains *four gospels*, not just one.[3] The fact that there is a plurality of gospels means that they can function in at least two ways. On the one hand, they can be *mutually reinforcing*—multiple testimonies to the nature of Christian discipleship seen through the respective gospel stories of the life of Jesus. The repetition is not redundant from a canonical perspective. Instead, the repetition is emphatic and intensifying. It points again and again to what is important, in a way that has the potential to overcome resistance in the reader or listener and allow him or her to see beneath the surface of things or to see things in a new way.

For example, the four narratives of the Passion leave us in no doubt that Christian spirituality involves the believer in a struggle with the forces of evil, the consequence of which may well be that the believer becomes a victim of those forces. The four accounts of Jesus' anointing by a woman highlight in various aspects the subversive nature of true Christian devotion and the radical inclusiveness of the Christian way. The multiple accounts of the temptation, in the synoptics, leave an indelible impression that the call to the service of God is not accompanied by guarantees of immunity from testing or trial: in fact, the vocation and the testing go together. The multiple accounts of the Gethsemane episode in the synoptics, together with Jesus' prayer to the Father in John 17, are mutually reinforcing reminders that both perseverance in times of crisis and preparation for death cannot be sustained adequately apart from prayer to God as 'Father'. The numerous accounts of the miraculous feedings of the multitudes by Jesus—and here, there are multiple accounts within single gospels (i.e. Mark and Matthew) as well as between all four!—draw attention most emphatically to the christological claim at the heart of Christian spirituality: that true life as the people of God is to be found by accepting the nourishment which comes from Jesus. Such examples could be multiplied. They show how important is repetition from one gospel to another for bringing to our attention what our obtuseness and hardness of heart might otherwise prevent us from seeing.

On the other hand, as well as being mutually reinforcing, the four gospels can be *mutually correcting*: an apparent intolerance here being counterbalanced by an inclusivism there, an emphasis

146

on control and discipline there contrasting with a focus on freedom and joy elsewhere, and so on.[4] There is, in other words, an inherent pluralism in the phenomenon of four gospels which allows them to function in an inspirational and fertile way for different kinds of people and in different kinds of circumstances. With four gospels, no one can claim to have said the last word on a subject, no one can claim to have given *the* definitive interpretation. With four gospels, it will always be a matter of weighing one account against another and discerning which, if any, brings one closest to the truth or shows one most clearly the way to go. With four gospels, there is always the possibility of delighting in the variety of colours in what Robert Morgan calls 'the biblical paint-box'[5] out of which the reader draws images of faith.

It may be, for example, that a spirituality nourished primarily by a gospel which sets faith in opposition to 'works of the law', and where the emphasis is on freedom and the life of the Spirit—as may be said of a Mark or a Paul, for instance—needs to be supplemented by the spirituality of a Matthew, where the emphasis is on the demand that faith find expression in bearing the good fruit which comes from active obedience to the commandments of Jesus. It may be, to give a second example, that the 'muscular Christianity' called for in Matthew is felt by some to be too directive, too lacking in scope for creativity and spontaneity, too much like an attempt to cover every exigency in advance. In such a case, the Fourth Gospel, with its simple but profound emphasis on love for Jesus and abiding in Jesus and being the friend of Jesus, may be a helpful corrective. Yet again, the stark and virtually unmitigated severity of Mark's spiritual vision, which focuses so single-mindedly upon going the way of the cross, may appear to foster a self-immolation which fails to do justice to the legitimate needs of the self for true personal fulfilment and growth towards integrity. In this case, the greater joyfulness and world-affirming character of Luke-Acts, with its commitment to historical development and its vision of the struggle and triumph of the gospel in the public domain, may function as a necessary supplement. Or, to give a final instance, the Fourth Gospel's emphasis on the individual and his or her personal faith-relationship to Jesus over against a hostile world where the darkness of unbelief reigns, may for some feel too

147

otherworldy, too individualistic, too monochrome in its view of the world. In such a case, the spirituality of the synoptics, with their stronger dimension of public proclamation, their summons to Israel and the nations to repentance and obedience to the will of God, and their more evident concern for the poor and needy, may provide a perspective lacking in John.

The canonical gospels can justly be interpreted as *classics* of Christian spirituality. They are classics because they do not wear thin upon repeated reading and hearing. On the contrary, they richly repay our constant return to them—by the information they impart, the emotions they stir, the images they evoke, the tensions they generate, and the direct, existential invitation to respond to the love of God in Christ which they offer. They also deserve our constant return, because it is they which have done so much to sustain and nourish the Christian tradition and the Christian community. It is in the worship of the church and the service of the church that the spirituality of the gospels comes into its own. It is in worship and service that men and women discover the truth of that spirituality and are enabled to bear witness to it.

Notes

1. Cf. S. Hauerwas and S. Long, 'Interpreting the Bible as a Political Act', *Religion and Intellectual Life*, VI (1989), pp. 134–42.
2. Among the many helpful works relevant to such an investigation, I would mention: R.J. Banks, *Jesus and the Law in the Synoptic Tradition* (Cambridge: Cambridge University Press, 1975); J.D.G. Dunn, *Jesus and the Spirit* (London: SCM Press, 1975), esp. Part One; M. Hengel, *The Charismatic Leader and his Followers* (ET, Edinburgh: T. & T. Clark, 1981); J. Jeremias, *New Testament Theology, Volume I* (ET, London: SCM Press, 1971); J. Riches, *Jesus and the Transformation of Judaism* (London: Darton, Longman & Todd, 1980); E.P. Sanders, *Jesus and Judaism* (London: SCM Press, 1985); and G. Vermes, *Jesus the Jew* (London: Collins, 1973).
3. See further, R. Morgan, 'The Hermeneutical Significance of Four Gospels', in J.L. Mays, ed., *Interpreting the Gospels* (Philadelphia: Fortress, 1981), pp. 41–54.
4. See further, Mary D'Angelo, 'Images of Jesus and the Christian Call in the Gospels of Luke and John', *Spirituality Today*, 37 (1985), pp. 196–212, noting esp. the conclusion on p. 211: 'Thus in the four Gospels we find four invitations that complement and correct each other.'
5. Morgan, 'Four Gospels', p. 52.

BIBLIOGRAPHY

Achtemeier, P.J., '"He Taught Them Many Things": Reflections on Marcan Christology', *Catholic Biblical Quarterly*, 42 (1980), pp. 465–81.

Achtemeier, P.J., 'Resources for Pastoral Ministry in the Synoptic Gospels', in E.E. Shelp and R. Sutherland, eds., *A Biblical Basis for Ministry* (Philadelphia, Fortress, 1981), pp. 145–85.

Achtemeier, P.J., 'The Lukan Perspective on the Miracles of Jesus: A Preliminary Sketch', in C.H. Talbert, ed., *Perspectives on Luke-Acts* (Edinburgh, T. & T. Clark, 1978), pp. 153–67.

Banks, R.J., *Jesus and the Law in the Synoptic Tradition*. Cambridge, Cambridge University Press, 1975.

Barrett, C.K., *Luke the Historian in Recent Study*. Philadelphia, Fortress, 1970.

Barrett, C.K., *The Gospel according to John*. London, SPCK, 1978².

Barton, S.C., 'The *Acts of the Apostles* as Evidence of the Relations between the Early Christian Communities and Roman Authority', *Ancient Society: Resources for Teachers*, 6 (Sydney, Macquarie University, 1976), pp. 120–41.

Barton, S.C., 'Roman Attitudes to Christianity and the Correspondence of Pliny' *Ancient Society: Resources for Teachers*, 6 (Sydney, Macquarie University, 1976), pp. 142–50.

Barton, S.C., 'Mark as Narrative: The Story of the Anointing Woman (Mk 14:3–9)', *Expository Times*, 102/8 (1991), pp. 230–4.

Barton, S.C., 'Women, Jesus and the Gospels', in R. Holloway, ed., *Who Needs Feminism? Men Respond to Sexism in the Church* (London, SPCK, 1991), pp. 32–58.

Barton, S.C., *Discipleship and Family Ties According to Mark and Matthew* (Ph.D. Thesis, King's College London, 1991; forthcoming, Cambridge University Press).

Barton, S.C., 'The Communal Dimension of Earliest Christianity', *Journal of Theological Studies* (forthcoming, 1992).

Bassler, J.M., 'Mixed Signals: Nicodemus in the Fourth Gospel', *Journal of Biblical Literature*, 108 (1989), pp. 635–46.

Beck, B.E., '"Imitatio Christi" and the Lucan Passion Narrative', in W. Horbury and B. McNeil, eds., *Suffering and Martyrdom in the New Testament* (Cambridge, Cambridge University Press, 1981), pp. 28–47.

149

Beck, B.E., 'Gethsemane in the Four Gospels', *Epworth Review*, 15 (1988), pp. 57–65.

Beck, B.E., *Christian Character in the Gospel of Luke*. London, Epworth, 1989.

Bernadicou, P.J., 'The Spirituality of Luke's Travel Narrative', *Review for Religious*, 36 (1977), pp. 455–66.

Best, E., *Following Jesus: Discipleship in the Gospel of Mark*. Sheffield, JSOT, 1981.

Bornkamm, G., 'The Risen Lord and the Earthly Jesus: Matthew 28:16–20', in J.M. Robinson, ed., *The Future of Our Religious Past* (London, SCM Press, 1971), pp. 203–29.

Brown, R.E., *The Gospel according to John I-XII*. London, Chapman, 1972.

Brown, R.E., *The Gospel according to John XIII-XXI*. London, Chapman, 1972.

Brown, R.E., *The Birth of the Messiah*. London, Chapman, 1977.

Brown, R.E., *The Community of the Beloved Disciple*. London, Chapman, 1979.

Brown, R.E., *The Churches the Apostles Left Behind*. New York, Paulist Press, 1984.

Burge, G.M., *The Anointed Community: The Holy Spirit in the Johannine Tradition*. Grand Rapids, Eerdmans, 1987.

Cassem, N.H., 'A Grammatical and Contextual Inventory of the Use of *kosmos* in the Johannnine Corpus', *New Testament Studies*, 19 (1972–3), pp. 81–91.

Catchpole, D.R., 'The Fearful Silence of the Women at the Tomb: A Study in Marcan Theology', *Journal of Theology for Southern Africa*, 18 (1977), pp. 3–10.

Childs, B.S., *The New Testament as Canon: An Introduction*. London, SCM Press, 1984.

Collins, R.F., 'The Representative Figures of the Fourth Gospel', *Downside Review*, 94 (1976), pp. 26–46, 118–32.

Conzelmann, H., *The Theology of Saint Luke*. ET, London, Faber, 1960.

Countryman, L.W., *The Mystical Way in the Fourth Gospel*. Philadelphia, Fortress, 1987.

Cousins, E., ed., *World Spirituality: An Encyclopedic History of the Religious Quest*. New York, Crossroad, 1985ff., and London, SCM Press, 1989ff..

Crosby, M.H., *House of Disciples: Church, Economics and Justice in Matthew*. New York, Orbis, 1988.

Culpepper, R.A., 'Story and History in the Gospels', *Review & Expositor*, 81 (1984), pp. 467–78.

Dahl, N., 'The Johannine Church and History', in J. Ashton, ed., *The Interpretation of John* (London: SPCK, 1986), pp. 122–40.

150

D'Angelo, M., 'Images of Jesus and the Christian Call in the Gospels of Luke and John', *Spirituality Today*, 37 (1985), pp. 196–212.

D'Angelo, M., 'Women in Luke-Acts', *Journal of Biblical Literature*, 109 (1990), pp. 441–61.

Davies, W.D. and Allison, D.C., *The Gospel According to Saint Matthew*, vol. 1. Edinburgh, T. & T. Clark, 1988.

Dobschütz, E. von, 'Matthew as Rabbi and Catechist', in G.N. Stanton, ed., *The Interpretation of Matthew* (London: SPCK, 1983), pp. 19–29.

Donahue, J.R., 'A Neglected Factor in the Theology of Mark', *Journal of Biblical Literature*, 101 (1982), pp. 563–94.

Donaldson, T.L., *Jesus on the Mountain: A Study in Matthean Theology*. Sheffield, JSOT, 1985.

Downing, F.G., *Jesus and the Threat of Freedom*. London, SCM Press, 1987.

Drury, J., 'Mark 1.1–15: An Interpretation', in A.E. Harvey, ed., *Alternative Approaches to New Testament Study* (London: SCM Press, 1985), pp. 25–36.

Dunn, J.D.G., *Baptism in the Holy Spirit*. London, SCM Press, 1970.

Dunn, J.D.G., *Jesus and the Spirit*. London, SCM Press, 1975.

Dunn, J.D.G., *Christology in the Making*. London, SCM Press, 1980.

Dunn, J.D.G., 'Let John be John: A Gospel for its Time', in P. Stuhlmacher, ed., *Das Evangelium und Die Evangelien* (Tübingen: Mohr/Siebeck, 1983), pp. 310–39.

Dunn, J.D.G., 'Models of Christian Community in the New Testament', in D. Martin and P. Mullen, eds., *Strange Gifts? A Guide to Charismatic Renewal* (Oxford: Blackwell, 1984), pp. 1–18.

Ehrman, B.D. and Plunkett, M.A., 'The Angel and the Agony: The Textual Problem of Luke 22:43–44', *Catholic Biblical Quarterly*, 45 (1983), pp. 401–16.

Esler, P.F., *Community and Gospel in Luke-Acts*. Cambridge, Cambridge University Press, 1987.

Fitzmyer, J.A., 'The Ascension of Christ and Pentecost', *Theological Studies*, 45 (1984), pp. 409–40.

Fitzmyer, J.A., 'The Composition of Luke, Chapter 9', in C.H. Talbert, ed., *Perspectives on Luke-Acts* (Edinburgh, T. & T. Clark, 1978), pp. 139–52.

Fitzmyer, J.A., *Luke the Theologian: Aspects of his Teaching*. London, Chapman, 1989.

Fraade, S.D., 'Ascetical Aspects of Ancient Judaism', in A. Green, ed., *Jewish Spirituality from the Bible through the Middle Ages* (London, SCM Press, 1989), pp. 253–88.

France, R.T., 'Mark and the Teaching of Jesus', in R.T. France and D. Wenham, eds., *Gospel Perspectives*, vol. 1 (Sheffield, JSOT, 1980), pp. 101–36.

Garner, C., 'What on Earth is Spirituality?', in J. Robson and D.

THE SPIRITUALITY OF THE GOSPELS

Lonsdale, eds., *Can Spirituality Be Taught?* (London, ACATE and BCC, no date), pp. 1–8.

Gerhardsson, B., *The Ethos of the Bible.* ET, London, Darton, Longman & Todd, 1982.

Graham, H., 'A Passion Prediction for Mark's Community: Mark 13:9–13', *Biblical Theology Bulletin*, XVI (1986), pp. 18–22.

Grant, P., *Reading the New Testament.* London, Macmillan, 1989.

Guelich, R.A., *Mark 1–8:26.* Dallas, Word Books, 1989.

Gundry, R.H., *Matthew: A Commentary on his Literary and Theological Art.* Grand Rapids, Eerdmans, 1982.

Hauerwas, S., and Long, S., 'Interpreting the Bible as a Political Act', *Religion and Intellectual Life*, 6 (1989), pp. 134–42.

Hellholm, D., ed., *Apocalypticism in the Mediterranean World and the Near East.* Tübingen, Mohr/Siebeck, 1983.

Hengel, M., *The Charismatic Leader and His Followers.* ET, Edinburgh, T. & T. Clark, 1981.

Hood, R.T., 'The Genealogies of Jesus', in A. Wikgren, ed., *Early Christian Origins* (Chicago, Quadrangle, 1961), pp. 1–15.

Hooker, M., *The Message of Mark.* London, Epworth, 1983.

Houlden, J.L., *Ethics and the New Testament.* London, Mowbray, 1973.

Houlden, J.L., *Backward Into Light:The Passion and Resurrection of Jesus according to Matthew and Mark.* London, SCM Press, 1987.

Hultgren, A.J., 'The Johannine Footwashing (13:1–11) as Symbol of Eschatological Hospitality', *New Testament Studies*, 28 (1982), pp. 539–46.

Hurtado, L.W., *One God, One Lord: Early Christian Devotion and Ancient Jewish Monotheism.* Philadelphia, Fortress, 1988.

Iersel, B.M.F. van, 'The gospel according to st. Mark—written for a persecuted community?', *Nederlands Theologisch Tijdschrift*, 34 (1980), pp. 15–36.

Jeremias, J., *New Testament Theology*, vol. 1. ET, London, SCM Press, 1971.

Johnson, L.T., *Sharing Possessions.* London, SCM Press, 1986.

Johnson, L.T., 'The New Testament's Anti-Jewish Slander and the Conventions of Ancient Polemic', *Journal of Biblical Literature*, 108 (1989), pp. 419–41.

Jones, C., Wainwright, G., Yarnold, E., eds., *The Study of Spirituality.* London, SPCK, 1986.

Jonge, M. de, *Jesus: Stranger from Heaven.* Missoula, Scholars Press, 1977.

Karris, R.J., 'Missionary Communities: A New Paradigm for the Study of Luke-Acts', *Catholic Biblical Quarterly*, 41 (1979), pp. 80–97.

Karris, R.J., 'Poor and Rich: The Lukan *Sitz im Leben*', in C.H. Talbert, ed., *Perspectives on Luke-Acts* (Edinburgh, T. & T. Clark, 1978), pp. 112–25.

Karris, R.J., 'Luke's Soteriology of With-ness', *Currents in Theology and Mission*, 12 (1985), pp. 346–52.

Käsemann, E., *Jesus Means Freedom*. ET, Philadelphia, Fortress, 1972.

Käsemann, E., *The Testament of Jesus: A Study of the Gospel of John in the Light of Chapter 17*. ET, London, SCM Press, 1968.

Keck, L.E., 'Ethics in the Gospel According to Matthew', *Illif Review*, 40/4 (1984), pp. 39–56.

Kermode, F., *The Sense of an Ending*. London, Oxford University Press, 1966.

Kermode, F., *The Genesis of Secrecy*. Cambridge, Mass., Harvard University Press, 1979.

Kierkegaard, S., *Attack Upon "Christendom"*. ET, Princeton, Princeton University Press, 1968.

Kingsbury, J.D., *Matthew: Structure, Christology and Kingdom*, London, SPCK, 1976.

Kingsbury, J.D., 'The Verb *Akolouthein* ("To Follow") as an Index of Matthew's View of his Community', *Journal of Biblical Literature*, 97 (1978), pp. 56–73.

Kingsbury, J.D., *Conflict in the Gospel of Mark*. Philadelphia, Fortress, 1990.

Koenig, J., *New Testament Hospitality*. Philadelphia, Fortress, 1985.

Lampe, G.W.H., 'Miracles in the Acts of the Apostles', in C.F.D. Moule, ed., *Miracles* (London, Mowbray, 1965), pp. 165–78.

Lampe, G.W.H., 'St. Peter's Denial', *Bulletin of the John Rylands Library*, 55 (1972–73), pp. 346–68.

Lightfoot, R.H., *The Gospel Message of Mark*. Oxford, Clarendon Press, 1950.

Lincoln, A.T., 'Matthew—A Story for Teachers?', in D.J.A. Clines *et al.*, eds., *The Bible in Three Dimensions* (Sheffield, JSOT, 1990), pp. 103–26.

Lindars, B., 'The persecution of Christians in John 15:18–16:4a', in W. Horbury and B. McNeil, eds., *Suffering and Martyrdom in the New Testament* (Cambridge, Cambridge University Press, 1981), pp. 48–69.

Luz, U., 'The Disciples in the Gospel According to Matthew', in G.N. Stanton, *The Interpretation of Matthew* (London, SPCK, 1983), pp. 98–128.

MacRae, G.W., '"Whom Heaven Must Receive Until The Time": Reflections on the Christology of Acts', *Interpretation*, XXVII (1973), pp. 151–65.

Malbon, E.S., *Narrative Space and Mythic Meaning Meaning in Mark*. New York, Harper & Row, 1986.

Malbon, E.S., 'Fallible Followers: Women and Men in the Gospel of Mark', in M.A. Tolbert, ed., *The Bible and Feminist Hermeneutics = SEMEIA*, 28 (1983), pp. 29–48.

Marcus, J., 'Mark 4:10–12 and Marcan Epistemology', *Journal of Biblical Literature*, 103 (1984), pp. 557–74.

Marshall, I.H., 'Luke and his "Gospel"', in P. Stuhlmacher, ed., *Das Evangelium und die Evangelien* (Tübingen, Mohr/Siebeck, 1983), pp. 289–307.

Martyn, J.L., *History and Theology in the Fourth Gospel*. Nashville, Abingdon, 1979².

Matera, F.J., *Passion Narratives and Gospel Theologies*. New York, Paulist Press, 1986.

McGann, D., *Journeying Within Transcendence: A Jungian Perspective on the Gospel of John*. London, Collins, 1989.

Meeks, W.A., 'The Man from Heaven in Johannine Sectarianism', in J. Ashton, *The Interpretation of John* (London, SPCK, 1986), pp. 141–73.

Meeks, W.A., *The Moral World of the First Christians*. London, SPCK, 1986.

Mello, A. de, *The Song of the Bird*. Gujarat, Anand Press, 1982.

Metzger, B.M., *A Textual Commentary on the Greek New Testament*. London, United Bible Societies, 1971.

Moberly, W., 'Proclaiming Christ Crucified: Some Reflections on the Use and Abuse of the Gospels', *Anvil*, 5 (1988), pp. 31–52.

Morgan, R., 'The Hermeneutical Significance of Four Gospels', in J.L. Mays, ed., *Interpreting the Gospels* (Philadelphia, Fortress, 1981), pp. 41–54.

Morgan, R. with Barton, J., *Biblical Interpretation*. Oxford, Oxford University Press, 1988.

Morrice, W., *Joy in the New Testament*. Grand Rapids, Eerdmans, 1985.

Moxnes, H., 'Meals and the New Community in Luke', *Svensk Exegetisk Arsbok*, 51–2 (1986–7), pp. 158–67.

Mursell, G., *Out of the Deep: Prayer as Protest*. London, Darton, Longman & Todd, 1989.

Neale, D.A., *None but the Sinners: Religious Categories in the Gospel of Luke*. Sheffield, JSOT, 1991.

Nickelsburg, G.W.E., 'Revealed Wisdom as a Criterion for Inclusion and Exclusion: From Jewish Sectarianism to Early Christianity', in J. Neusner and E.S. Frerichs, eds., *"To See Ourselves as Others See Us": Christians, Jews, "Others" in Late Antiquity* (Chico, Scholars Press, 1985), pp. 73–91.

Okure, T., *The Johannine Approach to Mission: A Contextual Study of John 4:1–42*. Tübingen, Mohr/Siebeck, 1988.

Orton, D.E., *The Understanding Scribe*. Sheffield, Sheffield Academic Press, 1989.

Overman, J.A., *Matthew's Gospel and Formative Judaism*. Minneapolis, Augsburg Fortress, 1990.

Painter, J., *John: Witness & Theologian*. London, SPCK, 1975.

Painter, J., 'Johannine Symbols: A Case Study in Epistemology', *Journal of Theology for Southern Africa*, 27 (1979), pp. 26–41.

BIBLIOGRAPHY

Pamment, M., 'Path and Residence Metaphors in the Fourth Gospel'. *Theology*, 88 (1985), pp. 118–25.

Przybylski, B., *Righteousness in Matthew and his World of Thought.* Cambridge, Cambridge University Press, 1980.

Quesnell, Q., '"Made Themselves Eunuchs for the Sake of the Kingdom of Heaven" (Matt 19,12)', *Catholic Biblical Quarterly*, 30 (1968), pp. 335–58.

Rensberger, D., *Johannine Faith and Liberating Community*. Philadelphia, Westminster, 1988; London, SPCK, 1989.

Richards, H.J., *The First Christmas: What Really Happened?* London. Mowbray, 1973.

Riches, J., *Jesus and the Transformation of Judaism.* London, Darton, Longman & Todd, 1980.

Rhoads, D. and Michie, D., *Mark as Story.* Philadelphia, Fortress, 1982.

Russell, D.S., *The Method and Message of Jewish Apocalyptic.* London, SCM Press, 1964.

Sanders, E.P., *Jesus and Judaism.* London, SCM Press, 1985.

Schlier, H., 'The State according to the New Testament', in his *The Relevance of the New Testament* (ET, London, Burns & Oates, 1968), pp. 215–38.

Schneider, S.M., 'The Footwashing (John 13:1–20): An Experiment in Hermeneutics', *Catholic Biblical Quarterly*, 43 (1981), pp. 76–92.

Schütz, J.H., 'Ethos of Early Christianity', in *Interpreters Dictionary of the Bible—Supplementary Volume*, pp. 289–94.

Schweizer, E., 'Observance of the Law and Charismatic Activity in Matthew', *New Testament Studies*, 16 (1970), pp. 213–30.

Schweizer, E., 'The Portrayal of the Life of Faith in the Gospel of Mark', in J.L. Mays, ed., *Interpreting the Gospels* (Philadelphia, Fortress, 1981), pp. 168–82.

Schweizer, E., 'Mark's Theological Achievement', in W. Telford, ed., *The Interpretation of Mark* (London, SPCK, 1985), pp. 42–63.

Segovia, F.F., *Love Relationships in the Johannine Tradition.* Chico, Scholars Press, 1982.

Shklar, J. N., 'Subversive Genealogies', in C. Geertz, ed., *Myth, Symbol and Culture* (New York, Norton, 1971), pp. 129–54.

Siker-Gieseler, J.S., 'Disciples and Discipleship in the Fourth Gospel: A Canonical Approach', *Studia Biblica et Theologica*, 10 (1980), pp. 199–227.

Smith, D.M., 'Johannine Christianity: Some Reflections on its Character and Delineation', *New Testament Studies*, 21 (1975), pp. 224–48.

Smith, D.M., 'Theology and Ministry in John', in E.E. Shelp and R. Sunderland, eds., *A Biblical Basis for Ministry* (Philadelphia, Westminster, 1981), pp. 186–238.

Sparks, H.F.D., 'The Doctrine of the Divine Fatherhood in the Gospels', in D.E. Nineham, ed., *Studies in the Gospels: Essays in Memory of R.H. Lightfoot* (Oxford, Blackwell, 1967), pp. 241–62

Stanton, G.N., 'The Gospel of Matthew and Judaism', *Bulletin of the John Rylands Library*, 66 (1984), pp. 264–84.

Stanton, G.N., *The Gospels and Jesus*. Oxford, Oxford University Press, 1989.

Stendahl, K., *'Quis et Unde?* An Analysis of Matthew 1–2', in G.N. Stanton, ed., *The Interpretation of Matthew* (London, SPCK, 1983), pp. 56–66.

Suggs, M.J., *Wisdom, Christology and Law in Matthew's Gospel*. Cambridge, Mass., Harvard University Press, 1970.

Swartley, W.M., 'The Structural Function of the Term 'Way' (*Hodos*) in Mark's Gospel', in W. Klassen, ed., *The New Way of Jesus* (Kansas, Faith and Life, 1980), pp. 73–86.

Talbert, C.H., *Reading Luke*. New York, Crossroad, 1982; London, SPCK, 1990.

Talbert, C.H., 'The Way of the Lukan Jesus: Dimensions of Lukan Spirituality', *Perspectives in Religious Studies*, 9 (1982), pp. 237–49.

Talbert, C.H., 'Discipleship in Luke-Acts', in F.F. Segovia, ed., *Discipleship in the New Testament* (Philadelphia, Fortress, 1985), pp. 62–75.

Tannehill, R.C., 'The Disciples in Mark: The Function of a Narrative Role', in W. Telford, ed., *The Interpretation of Mark* (London, SPCK, 1985), pp. 134–57.

Telford, W.R., *The Barren Temple and the Withered Tree*. Sheffield, JSOT, 1980.

Thompson, M.M., *The Humanity of Jesus in the Fourth Gospel*. Philadelphia, Fortress, 1988.

Thompson, W.G., *Matthew's Advice to a Divided Community*. Rome, Biblical Institute Press, 1970.

Thompson, W.G., *The Gospels for your Whole Life: Mark and John in Prayer and Study*. Minneapolis, Winston Press, 1983.

Trilling, W., *Das Wahre Israel*. Munich, Kosel, 1964³.

Trites, A.A., 'The Prayer Motif in Luke-Acts', in C.H. Talbert, ed., *Perspectives on Luke-Acts* (Edinburgh, T&T Clark, 1978), pp. 168–86.

Twelftree, G.H., *Christ Triumphant: Exorcism Then and Now*. London, Hodder & Stoughton, 1985.

Vanstone, W.H., *The Stature of Waiting*. London, Darton, Longman & Todd, 1982.

Verhey, A., *The Great Reversal: Ethics and the New Testament*. Grand Rapids, Eerdmans, 1984.

Vermes, G., *Jesus the Jew*. London, Collins, 1973.

Via, D.O, *Self-Deception and Wholeness in Paul and Matthew*. Minneapolis, Augsburg Fortress, 1990.

Wakefield, G.S., ed., *A Dictionary of Spirituality*. London, SCM Press, 1983.

Wakefield, G.S., 'Recent Books on Spirituality and their Trends', *Epworth Review*, 14/3 (1987), pp. 92–7.

Wiles, M.F., *The Spiritual Gospel: The Interpretation of the Fourth Gospel in the Early Church.* Cambridge, Cambridge University Press, 1960.

Weaver, D.J., *Matthew's Missionary Discourse: A Literary Critical Analysis.* Sheffield, JSOT, 1990.

Weeden, T.J., *Mark—Traditions in Conflict.* Philadelphia, Fortress, 1971.

Williams, R., *The Wound of Knowledge: Christian Spirituality from the New Testament to St John of the Cross.* London, Darton, Longman & Todd, 1990².

Winstanley, M.T., *Come and See: An Exploration into Christian Discipleship.* London, Darton, Longman & Todd, 1985.

Woll, D.B., *Johannine Christianity in Conflict.* Chico, Scholars Press, 1981.

INDEX

almsgiving 19, 20, 25, 39, 80, 97, 100, 101
angels 11, 32, 58, 73, 75, 91, 106
anti-Judaism 29–30, 136
apocalyptic 30, 43, 104, 123
apostasy 26, 28, 51, 86–7, 90, 121
asceticism 19
assurance 114, 120, 123–5

canon 3, 4, 5, 33, 65, 113, 146
casuistry 51–2, 54, 55, 65, 66, 73
celibacy 20
character/characterization 71, 82–3, 100–4, 128–30
charismatic 4, 31, 73, 130–3, 135, 145
community 5, 46, 116–18, 126, 132, 135, 138, 145, 148
conflict 60–1, 119, 121
conversion 1, 77–83, 84, 95, 98, 99, 100
counter-culture 60, 61
creation 9

discipleship 14, 49–52, 53, 55, 57, 60, 64, 89, 98, 99, 106, 107, 121, 138, 146

doubt 32–3

ecclesiology 27, 34, 39, 137–8
eschatology 34, 54–7, 58, 72–4, 77, 86, 102, 103, 124, 132
eternal life 2, 19, 114, 115, 118, 119, 132, 137, 138
ethics 1, 5, 29, 72, 134–5

faith 2, 3, 5, 15, 20, 29, 30, 31, 32, 33, 44–5, 47, 50, 60, 79, 81, 82, 83–7, 95, 105, 118, 119, 128, 129, 130, 133, 145, 147
fasting 1, 19, 20, 21, 25, 39
feminist spirituality 4
following (Jesus) 15, 16, 17, 18, 19, 29, 34, 49, 58–61, 65, 66, 97, 100, 126, 131
forgiveness 13, 23, 27, 28, 29, 79, 80, 81, 83, 84, 90, 91, 93, 95, 106
freedom 52, 84, 97, 99, 147

genealogy (of Jesus) 9–10, 11
grace 14, 15, 21, 22, 43, 72, 73, 74, 83, 84, 94, 97, 104, 115, 119, 131, 133

healing 14, 62, 84, 91, 93, 94, 97, 121–2, 133
historical method 3, 4, 5
history 120–3, 124
Holy Spirit 2, 11, 12, 14, 18, 43, 47, 57, 65, 71, 73, 77, 84, 88, 90, 91, 92–3, 94, 95, 96, 98, 113, 127, 130, 131, 132, 136, 138, 147
Holocaust 30
hospitality 25, 82, 102–3, 126
household relations 27, 51–2, 58, 60–1, 86, 100, 102, 103, 122, 129, 131
humility 13, 20, 29, 51, 79, 80, 89, 102, 123
humour 63
hypocrisy 20, 26–7, 30, 31, 85, 101

imitatio Christi 61–2, 94, 95
interiority 20ff, 23

joy 2, 63, 74–7, 82, 84, 87, 91, 95, 102–3, 147

kingdom of God/heaven 2, 10, 11, 13, 14, 15, 16, 20, 22, 24, 26, 28, 29, 30, 34, 39, 41, 42, 44, 45, 48, 51, 52, 54, 58, 63, 81, 84, 86, 100, 102, 103, 107, 118

law 25, 52–3, 136, 147

love 19, 22, 23, 25, 27, 28, 30, 31, 33, 44, 101–2, 115, 117, 118, 126, 129, 130, 134, 135, 139, 147, 148
learning 15–18

memory/remembering 120, 125
mercy 23, 83
messianism 72–3, 122–3
miracle 12, 41–2, 47, 48, 60, 64, 65, 84, 91, 94, 96, 104–6, 107, 124, 133, 146
mission 5, 12, 13, 14, 16, 17, 18, 21, 22, 25, 28, 30, 33, 45–6, 60, 74, 77, 93, 95, 96, 98, 105, 106, 107, 113, 122, 133, 135
mystery 43–4

name (of Jesus) 10, 11, 17, 93, 95, 96, 126, 133

obedience 14, 17, 18, 22, 24, 25, 28, 44, 46, 47, 87, 102, 147, 148

Paraclete 120, 124, 126, 131, 135, 138
particularity 135–7
persecution 30, 31, 46, 49, 50, 56, 63, 65, 86, 107, 125, 136
perseverance 2, 85–7, 89, 104, 107, 125–30, 146
politics 98–9, 121, 123, 135
possessions (and property) 100–1, 102
power 20, 62–3, 131–2
prayer 1, 12, 13, 18, 19, 20, 21, 23, 25, 39, 42, 45, 50, 54, 62, 71, 81, 86, 87–91, 92, 95,

103, 104, 106, 117, 126, 130, 133, 135, 145, 146

preaching 42, 54, 58, 93–4, 98, 107

presence (of God or Jesus) 1, 2, 10–14, 17, 18, 29, 33, 34, 39, 41, 43, 66, 73, 79, 88, 92–5, 113, 130, 144

providence 12, 18, 100

Qumran 17, 30, 119, 122

repentance 2, 3, 15, 71, 77–83, 87, 91, 95, 101, 148

revelation 20, 40, 43, 50, 99, 100, 113, 114, 115, 118, 119, 120, 122, 123, 124, 126, 131, 132, 134, 136

reward (and punishment) 13, 30–1

righteousness 15, 24–5, 28, 34, 39, 106

ritual 21, 23, 27

sacraments 127–8, 138

sacrifice 52

Satan 14, 18, 46, 57, 58, 86, 106, 128

scripture 3, 4, 5, 6, 28, 33, 34, 84, 94, 113, 117, 132, 134, 136, 144, 145

sectarianism 122, 135, 136

sermon on the mount/plain 12, 14, 15, 16, 17, 19, 24, 26, 30, 88, 100, 101, 134

sexual discipline 19–20

Shema 18, 19, 44

spirituality 1–4 and *passim*

story 28–9, 72

suffering 48–50, 57, 63, 94, 105

supernaturalism 104–6

symbolism 126–8, 136

temple (cult) 45, 54, 55, 57, 61, 64, 119, 120, 121, 131, 132, 136, 137, 138, 145

theodicy 46

theophany 11

Torah 17, 18, 28, 39, 119, 134, 137, 145

triumphalism 106–7

truth 6, 120, 123, 126, 127, 130

vigilance 55–6

vocation 57

waiting 62–3, 103–4

witness 2, 95–9, 115–16, 123, 124, 125

women 4, 10, 11, 23, 32, 44, 55, 60, 61, 62, 75, 78–9, 84, 91, 96–7, 101–2, 105, 116, 117, 124, 135, 137, 139, 146, 148

worship 6, 120, 132, 138, 148